Originally launched on Facebook, Rupert Fawcett's brilliantly observed, touchingly truthful Off The Leash cartoons have developed a huge daily following around the world.

This book brings together the very best of those cartoons, featuring the secret thoughts and conversations of dogs of every size, shape and breed. It is a celebration of our favourite belly-scratching, tail-chasing, bed-stealing canine friends – for dog lovers everywhere.

Off The Leash

THE SECRET LIFE OF DOGS

Rupert Fawcett

BOXTREE

First published 2013 by Boxtree
an imprint of Pan Macmillan, a division of Macmillan Publishers Limited
Pan Macmillan, 20 New Wharf Road, London N1 9RR
Basingstoke and Oxford
Associated companies throughout the world
www.panmacmillan.com

ISBN 978-1-4472-5084-5

1 3 5 7 9 8 6 4 2

A CIP catalogue record for this book is available from the British Library.

Printed and bound in China

Visit **www.panmacmillan.com** to read more about all our books
and to buy them. You will also find features, author interviews and
news of any author events, and you can sign up for e-newsletters
so that you're always first to hear about our new releases.

Foreword

I was brought up with dogs and have always found them comical as well as very lovable. About a year ago, I started drawing cartoons featuring talking dogs and was encouraged by friends to put them on a social media site. I then created an Off The Leash Facebook page and started posting one a day. I was amazed by the response and now have many thousands of people following the cartoons every day, all over the world. The cartoons appeal to all sorts of people, from passionate dog lovers who have eight sleeping on their bed at night, to people who don't have any pets at all, but can still identify with the characteristics. Let's face it, who doesn't like to be fed, have their tummy stroked and snooze on the sofa in the afternoon? This is my first Off The Leash compilation – I hope you enjoy it!

Rupert Fawcett

For Mandy

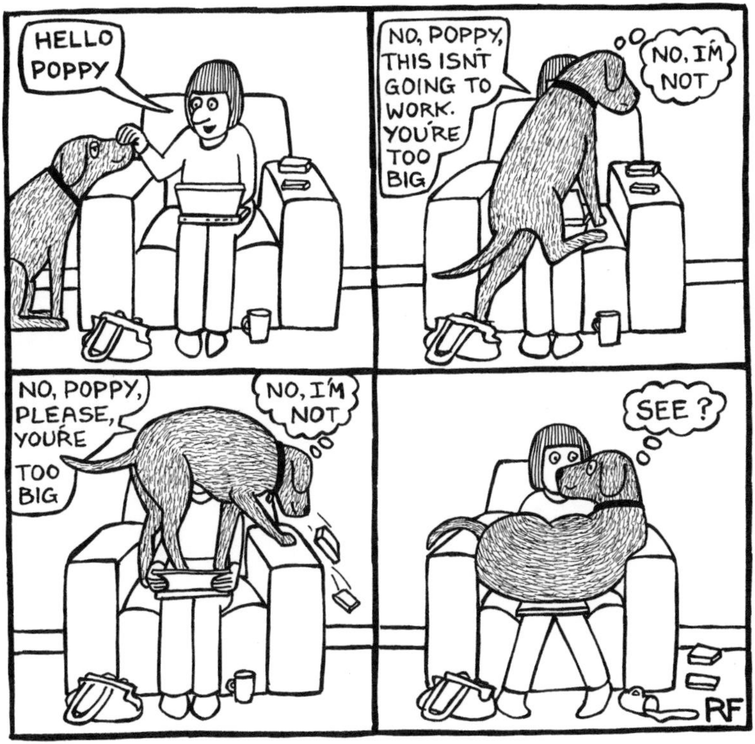
HELLO POPPY
NO, POPPY, THIS ISN'T GOING TO WORK. YOU'RE TOO BIG
NO, I'M NOT
NO, POPPY, PLEASE, YOU'RE TOO BIG
NO, I'M NOT
SEE?
RF

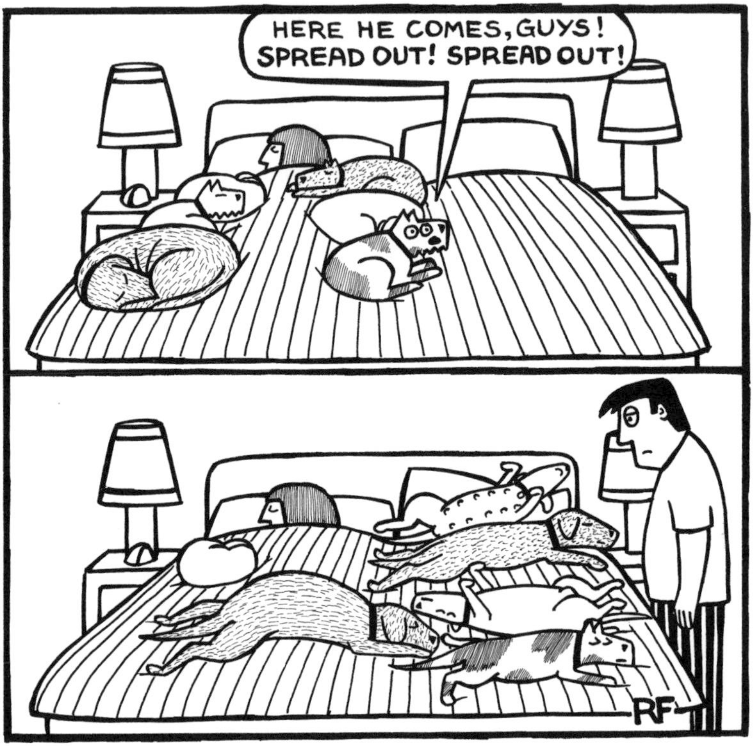
HERE HE COMES, GUYS! SPREAD OUT! SPREAD OUT!
RF

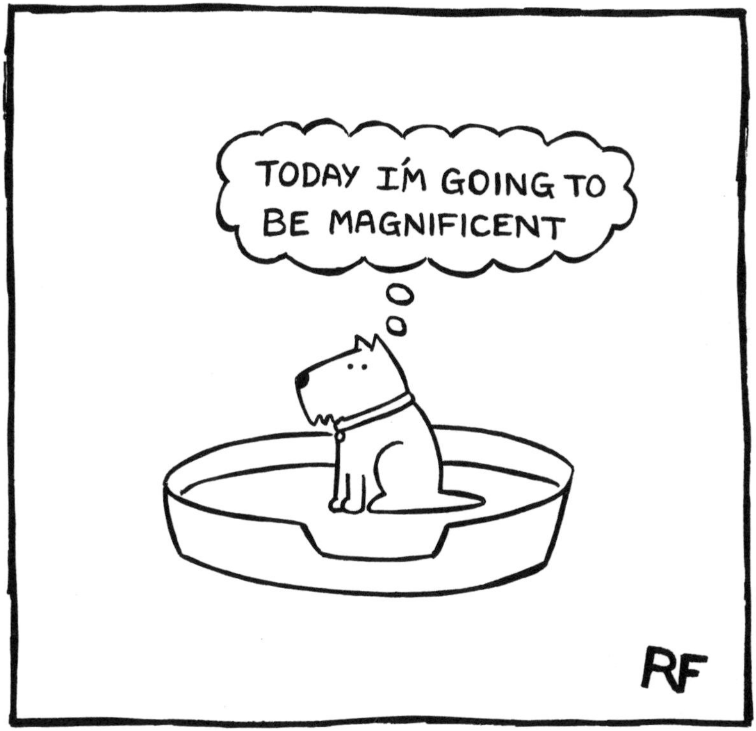
TODAY I'M GOING TO BE MAGNIFICENT
RF

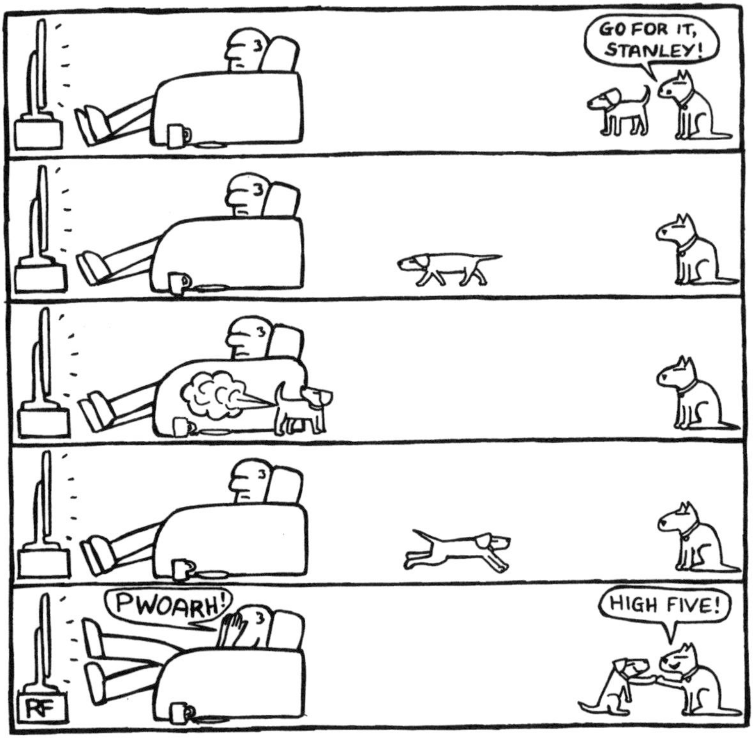
GO FOR IT, STANLEY!
PWOARH!
HIGH FIVE!
RF

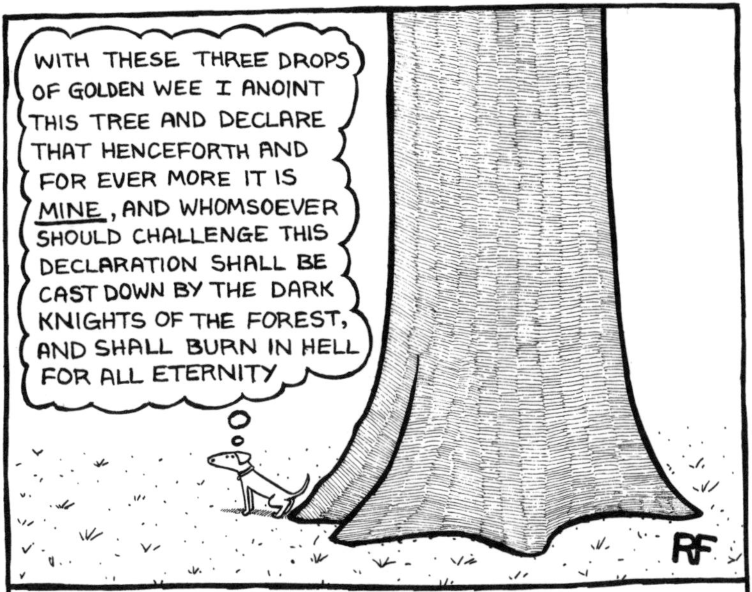
WITH THESE THREE DROPS OF GOLDEN WEE I ANOINT THIS TREE AND DECLARE THAT HENCEFORTH AND FOR EVER MORE IT IS MINE, AND WHOMSOEVER SHOULD CHALLENGE THIS DECLARATION SHALL BE CAST DOWN BY THE DARK KNIGHTS OF THE FOREST, AND SHALL BURN IN HELL FOR ALL ETERNITY
RF

PIPPA COULD SOMETIMES GET A BIT 'LORD OF THE RINGS' WHEN SHE WAS DOING HER BUSINESS

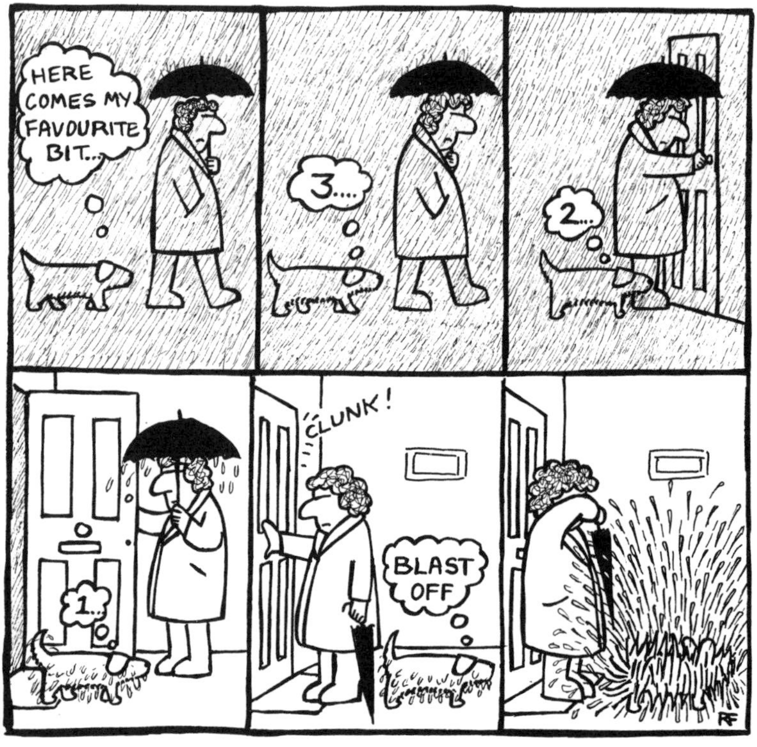
HERE COMES MY FAVOURITE BIT...
3....
2...
1...
CLUNK!
BLAST OFF
RF

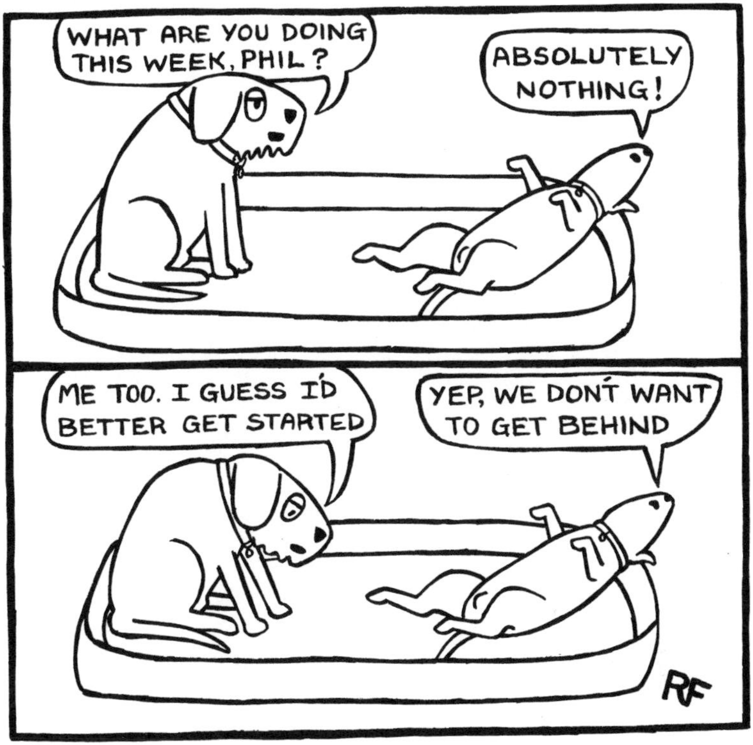
WHAT ARE YOU DOING THIS WEEK, PHIL?
ABSOLUTELY NOTHING!
ME TOO. I GUESS I'D BETTER GET STARTED
YEP, WE DON'T WANT TO GET BEHIND
RF

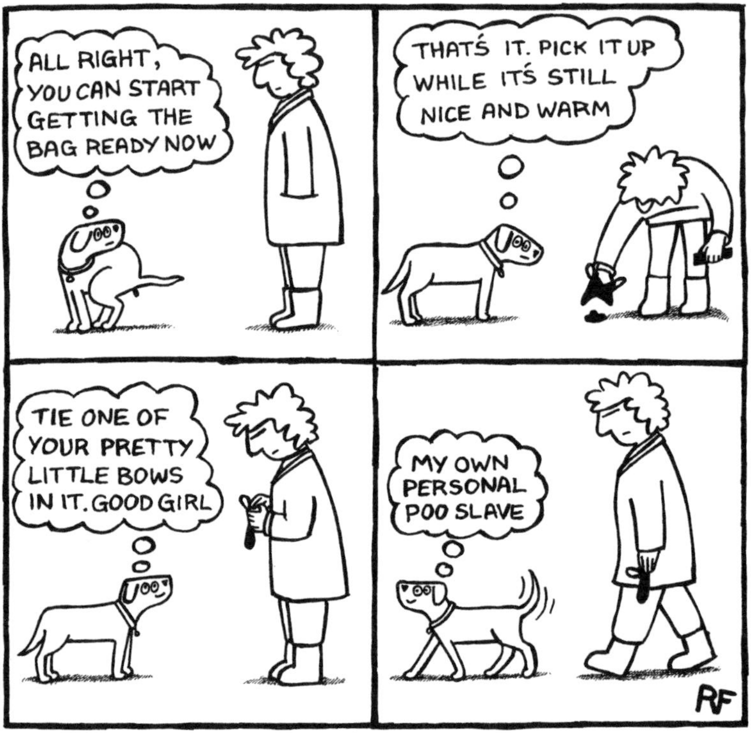
ALL RIGHT, YOU CAN START GETTING THE BAG READY NOW
THAT'S IT. PICK IT UP WHILE IT'S STILL NICE AND WARM
TIE ONE OF YOUR PRETTY LITTLE BOWS IN IT. GOOD GIRL
MY OWN PERSONAL POO SLAVE
RF

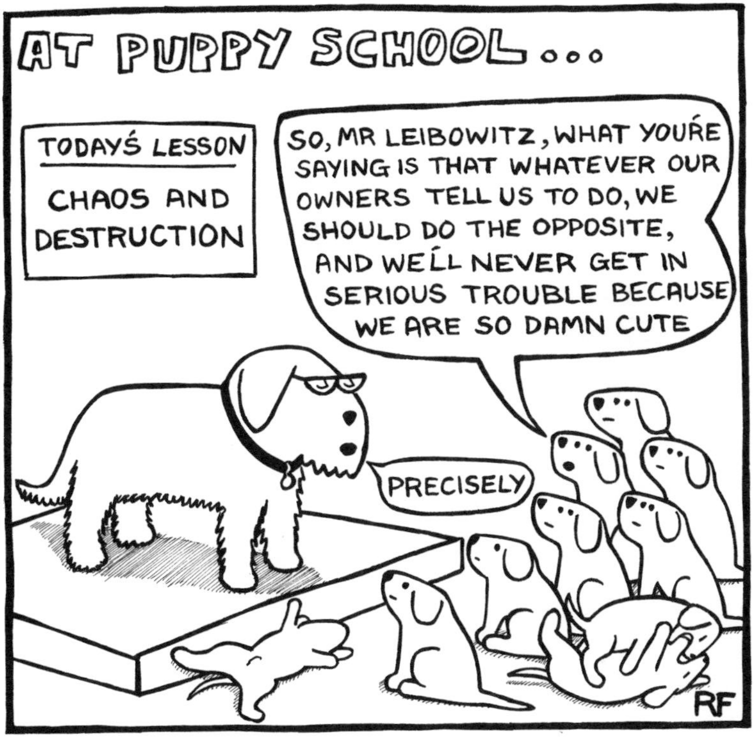
AT PUPPY SCHOOL...
TODAY'S LESSON
CHAOS AND DESTRUCTION
SO, MR LEIBOWITZ, WHAT YOU'RE SAYING IS THAT WHATEVER OUR OWNERS TELL US TO DO, WE SHOULD DO THE OPPOSITE, AND WE'LL NEVER GET IN SERIOUS TROUBLE BECAUSE WE ARE SO DAMN CUTE
PRECISELY
RF

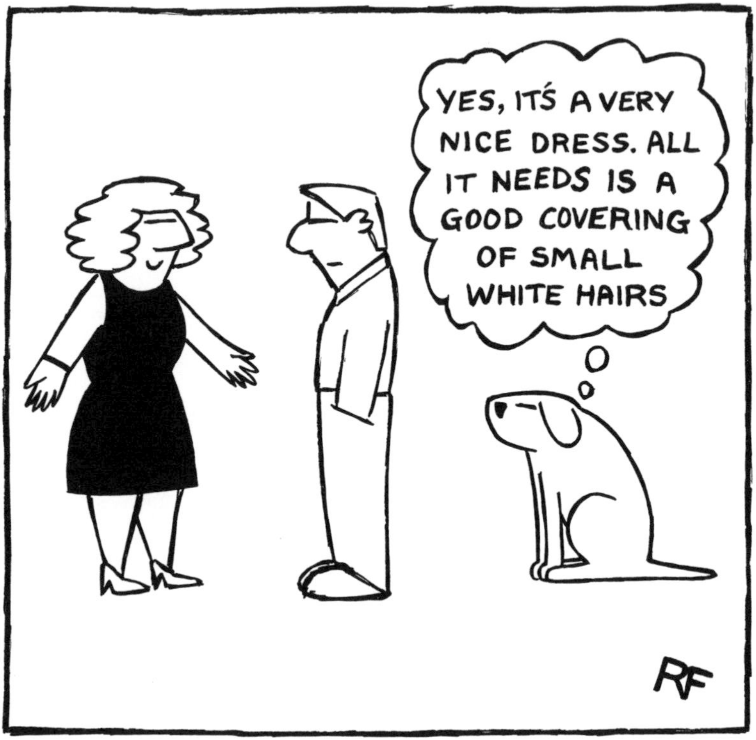
YES, IT'S A VERY NICE DRESS. ALL IT NEEDS IS A GOOD COVERING OF SMALL WHITE HAIRS
RF

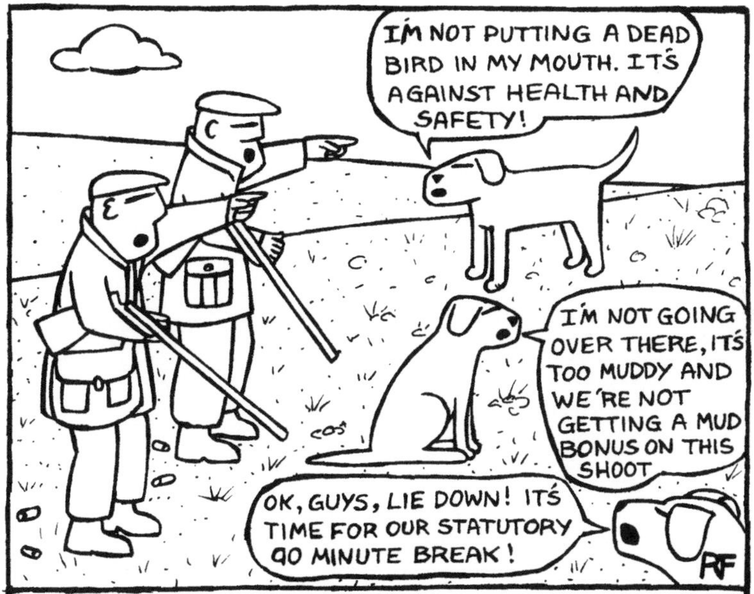
I'M NOT PUTTING A DEAD BIRD IN MY MOUTH. IT'S AGAINST HEALTH AND SAFETY!
I'M NOT GOING OVER THERE, IT'S TOO MUDDY AND WE'RE NOT GETTING A MUD BONUS ON THIS SHOOT
OK, GUYS, LIE DOWN! IT'S TIME FOR OUR STATUTORY 90 MINUTE BREAK!
RF

SHOOTING WAS NEVER THE SAME AGAIN AFTER THE FORMATION OF THE GUN DOGS UNION

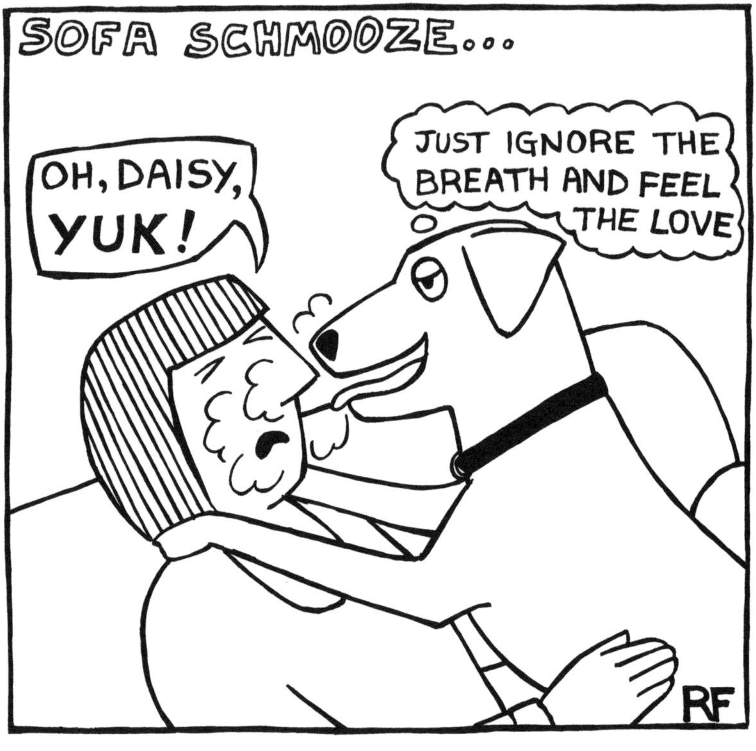
SOFA SCHMOOZE...
OH, DAISY, YUK!
JUST IGNORE THE BREATH AND FEEL THE LOVE
RF

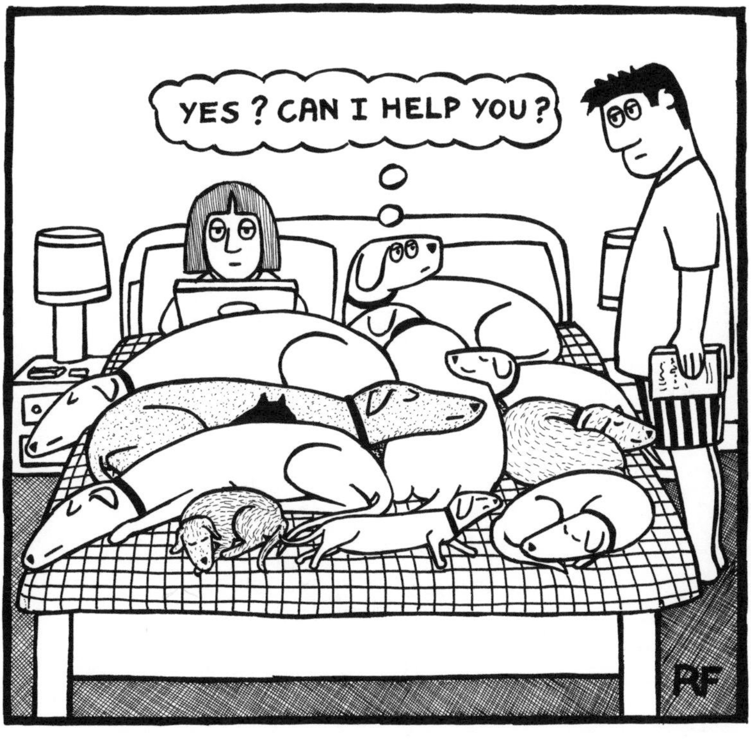
YES ? CAN I HELP YOU ?
RF

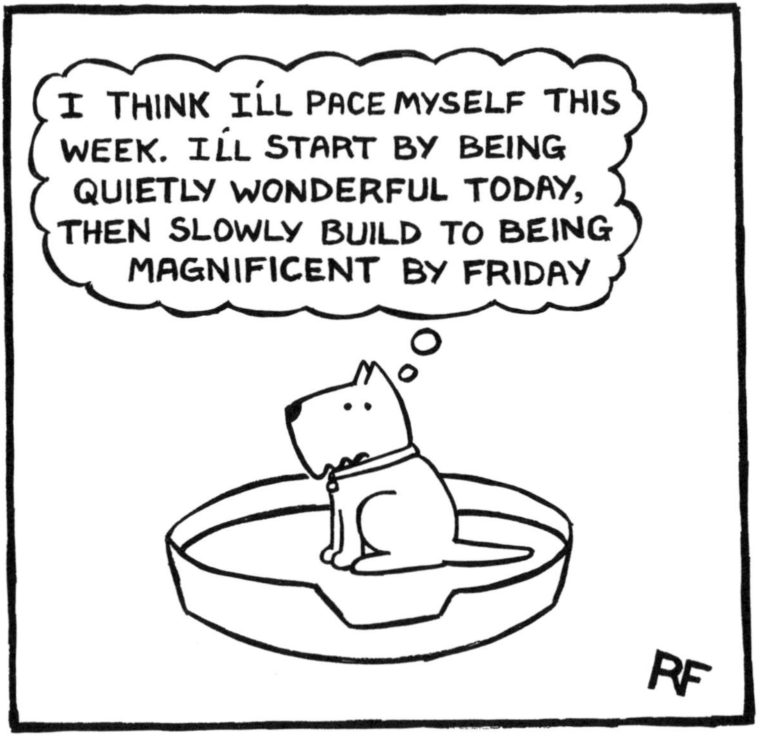
I THINK I'LL PACE MYSELF THIS WEEK. I'LL START BY BEING QUIETLY WONDERFUL TODAY, THEN SLOWLY BUILD TO BEING MAGNIFICENT BY FRIDAY
RF

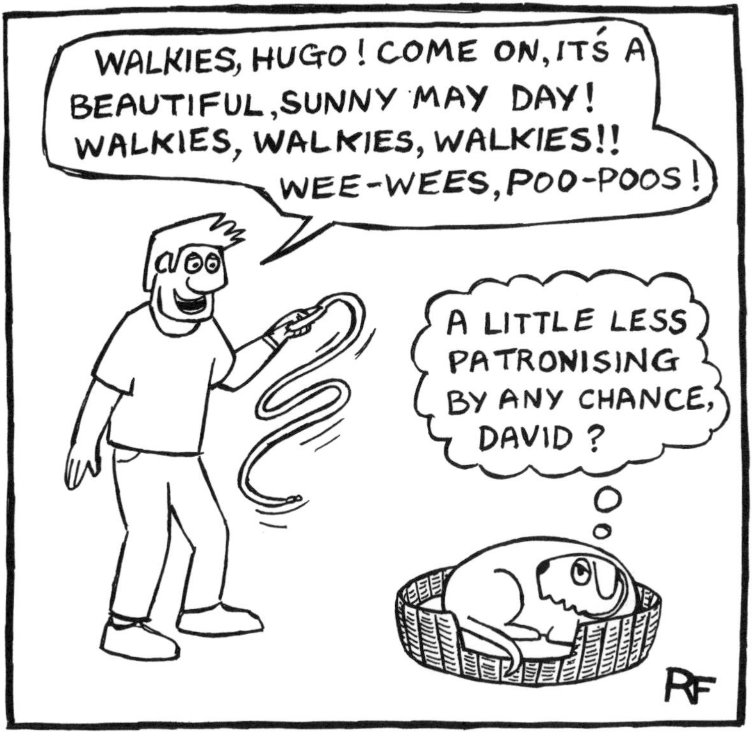
WALKIES, HUGO! COME ON, IT'S A BEAUTIFUL, SUNNY MAY DAY! WALKIES, WALKIES, WALKIES!! WEE-WEES, POO-POOS!
A LITTLE LESS PATRONISING BY ANY CHANCE, DAVID?
RF

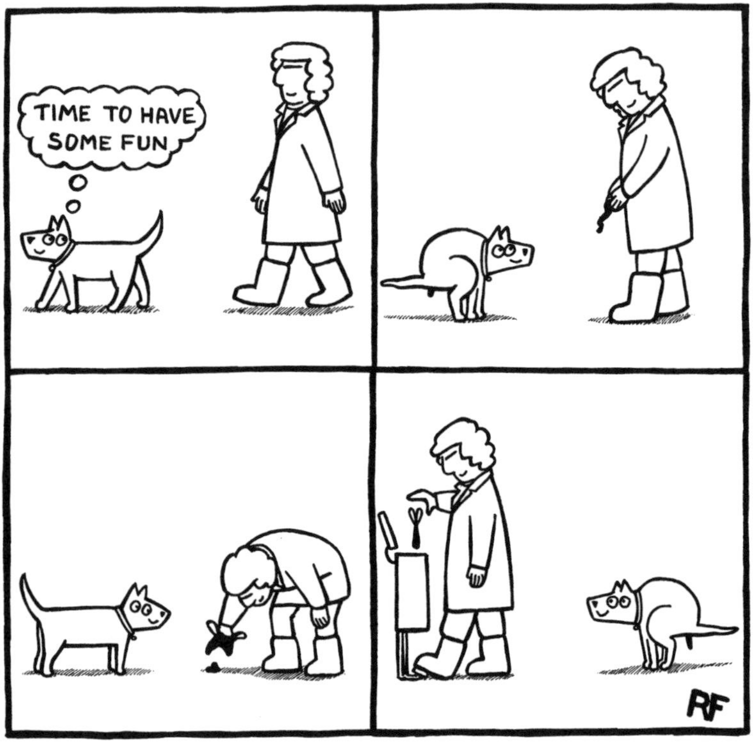
TIME TO HAVE SOME FUN
RF

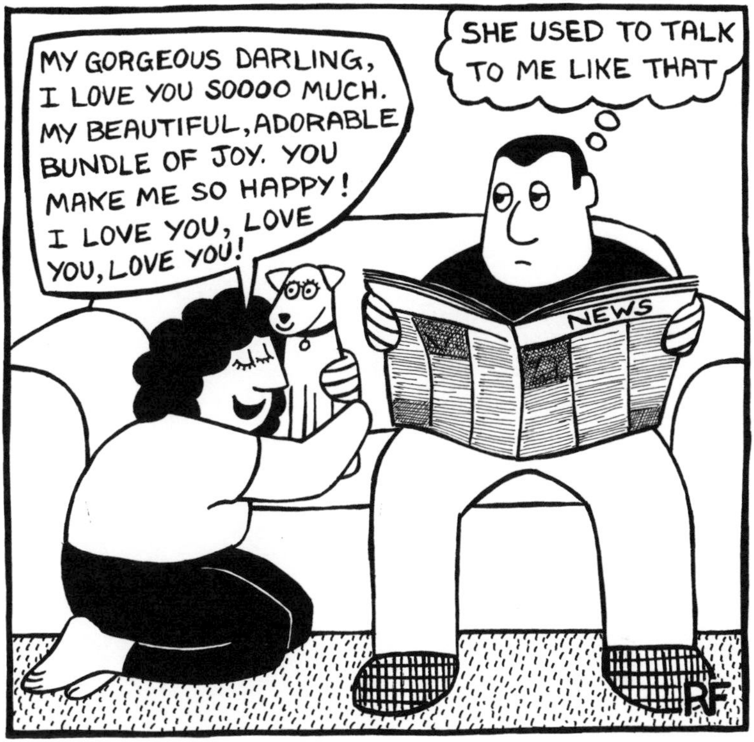
MY GORGEOUS DARLING, I LOVE YOU SOOOO MUCH. MY BEAUTIFUL, ADORABLE BUNDLE OF JOY. YOU MAKE ME SO HAPPY! I LOVE YOU, LOVE YOU, LOVE YOU!
SHE USED TO TALK TO ME LIKE THAT
NEWS
RF

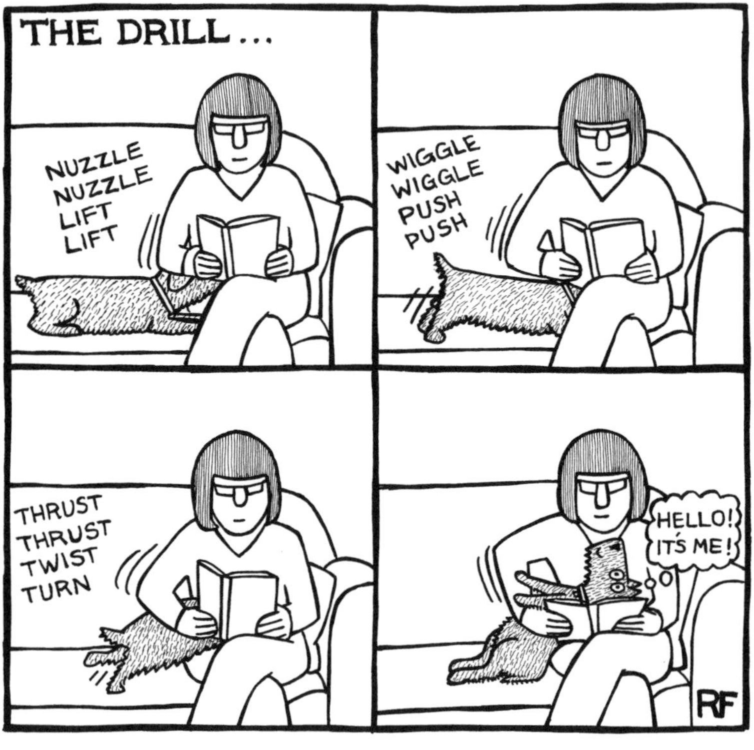
THE DRILL...
NUZZLE
NUZZLE
LIFT
LIFT
WIGGLE
WIGGLE
PUSH
PUSH
THRUST
THRUST
TWIST
TURN
HELLO!
IT'S ME!
RF

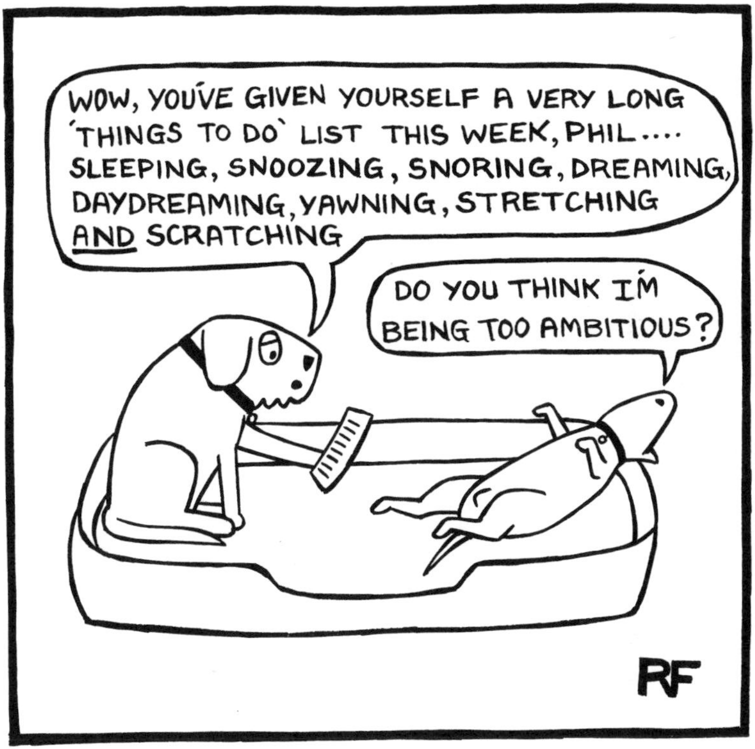
WOW, YOU'VE GIVEN YOURSELF A VERY LONG 'THINGS TO DO' LIST THIS WEEK, PHIL.... SLEEPING, SNOOZING, SNORING, DREAMING, DAYDREAMING, YAWNING, STRETCHING AND SCRATCHING
DO YOU THINK I'M BEING TOO AMBITIOUS?
RF

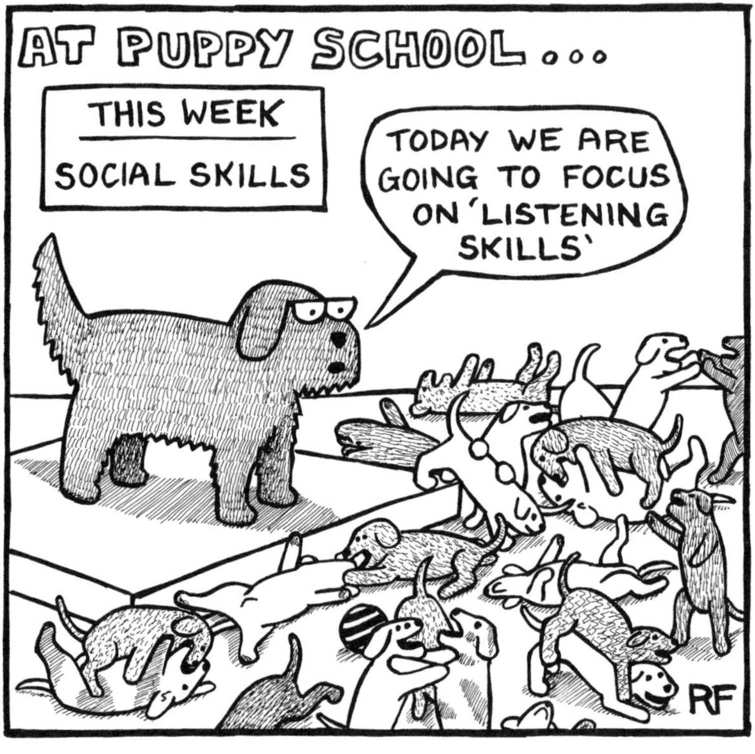
AT PUPPY SCHOOL...
THIS WEEK
SOCIAL SKILLS
TODAY WE ARE GOING TO FOCUS ON 'LISTENING SKILLS'
RF

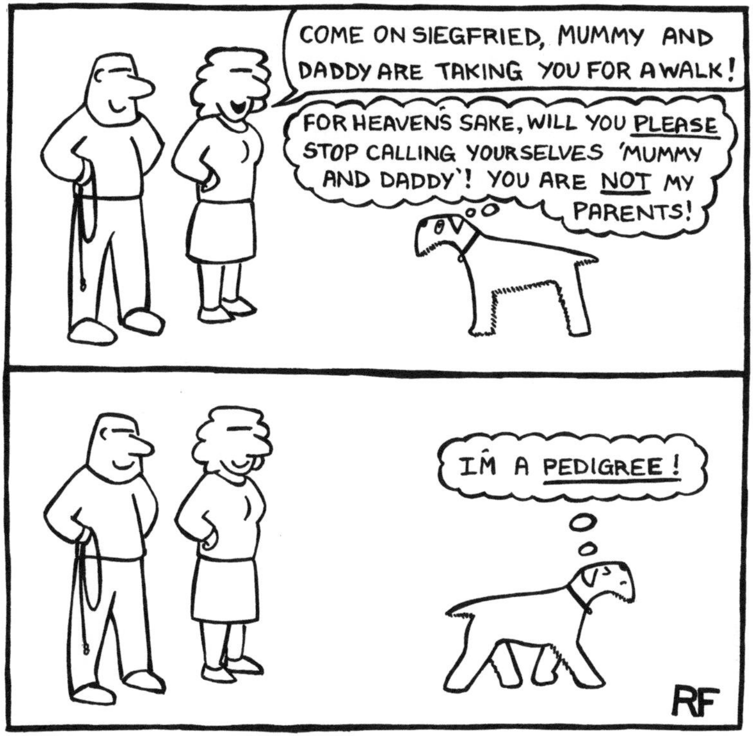
COME ON SIEGFRIED, MUMMY AND DADDY ARE TAKING YOU FOR A WALK!
FOR HEAVEN'S SAKE, WILL YOU PLEASE STOP CALLING YOURSELVES 'MUMMY AND DADDY'! YOU ARE NOT MY PARENTS!
I'M A PEDIGREE!
RF

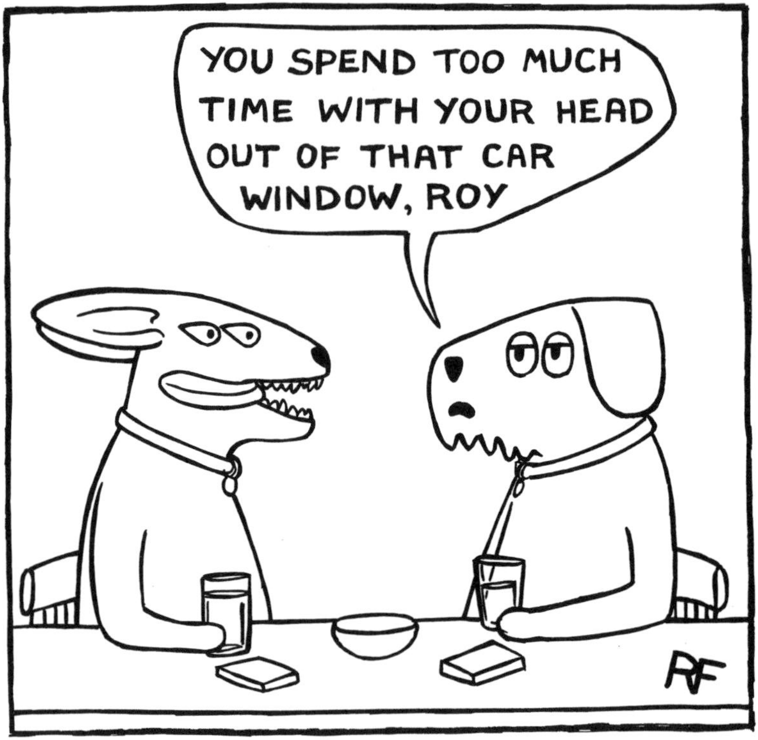
YOU SPEND TOO MUCH TIME WITH YOUR HEAD OUT OF THAT CAR WINDOW, ROY
RF

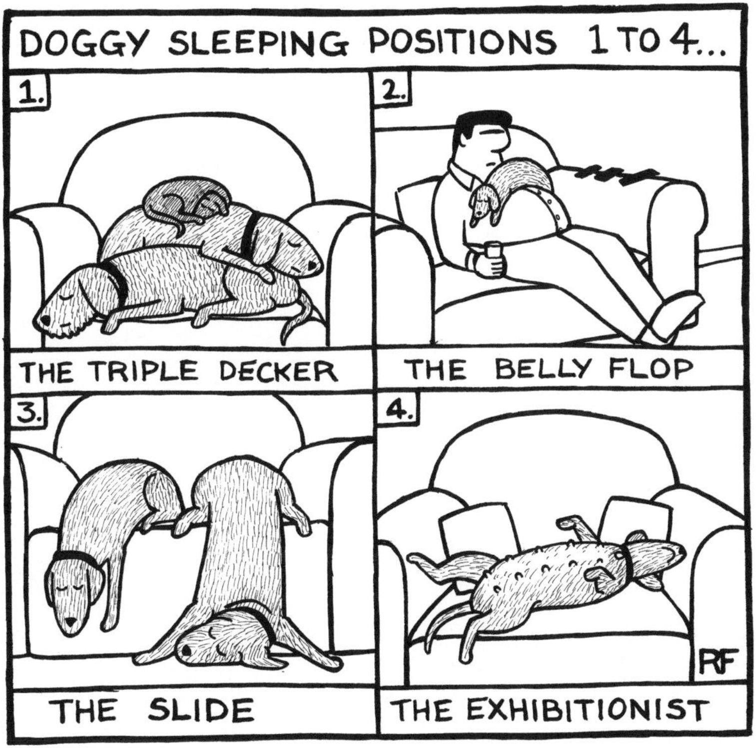
DOGGY SLEEPING POSITIONS 1 TO 4...
1.
THE TRIPLE DECKER
2.
THE BELLY FLOP
3.
THE SLIDE
4.
THE EXHIBITIONIST
RF

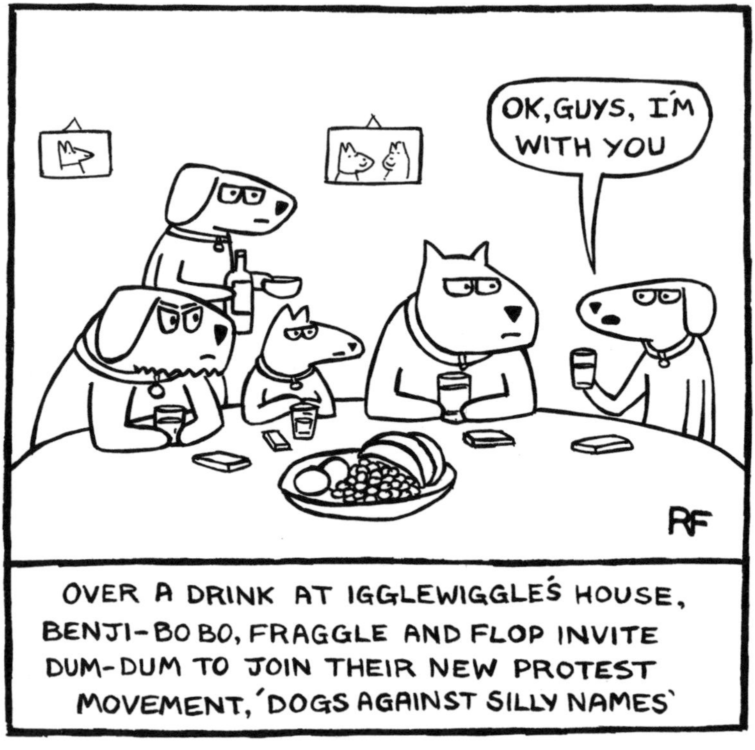
OK, GUYS, I'M WITH YOU
RF

OVER A DRINK AT IGGLEWIGGLE'S HOUSE, BENJI-BO BO, FRAGGLE AND FLOP INVITE DUM-DUM TO JOIN THEIR NEW PROTEST MOVEMENT, 'DOGS AGAINST SILLY NAMES'

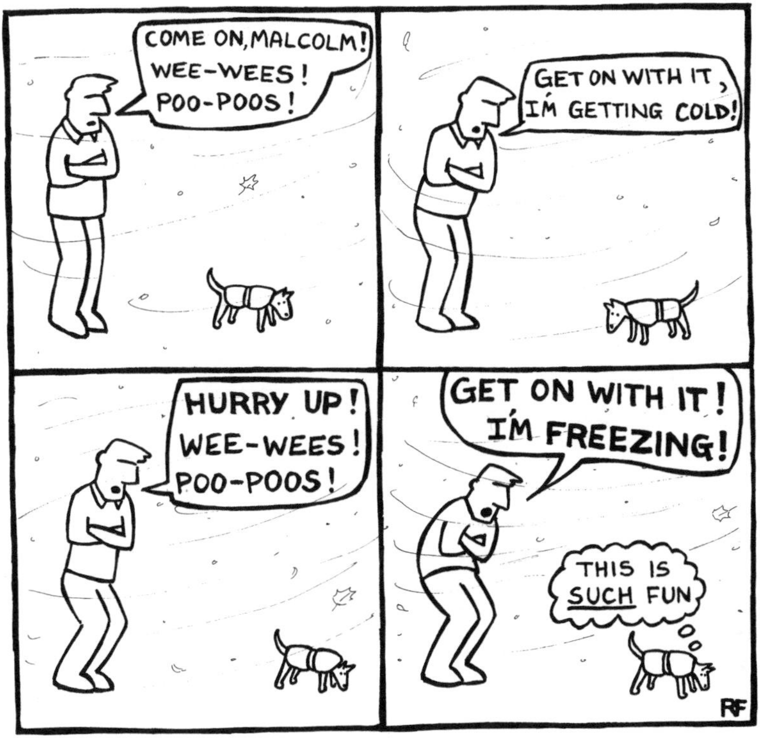
COME ON, MALCOLM! WEE-WEES! POO-POOS!
GET ON WITH IT, I'M GETTING COLD!
HURRY UP! WEE-WEES! POO-POOS!
GET ON WITH IT! I'M FREEZING!
THIS IS SUCH FUN
RF

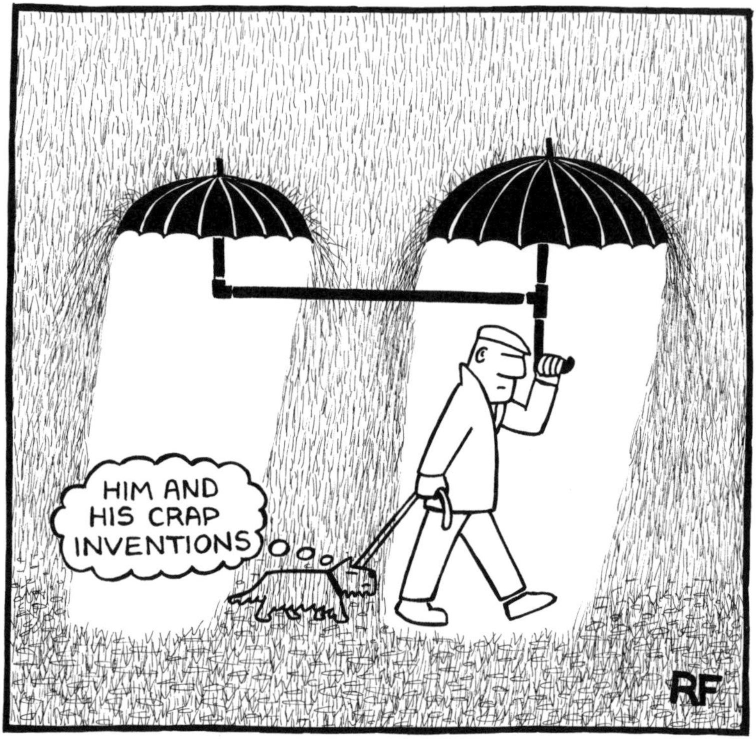
HIM AND HIS CRAP INVENTIONS
RF

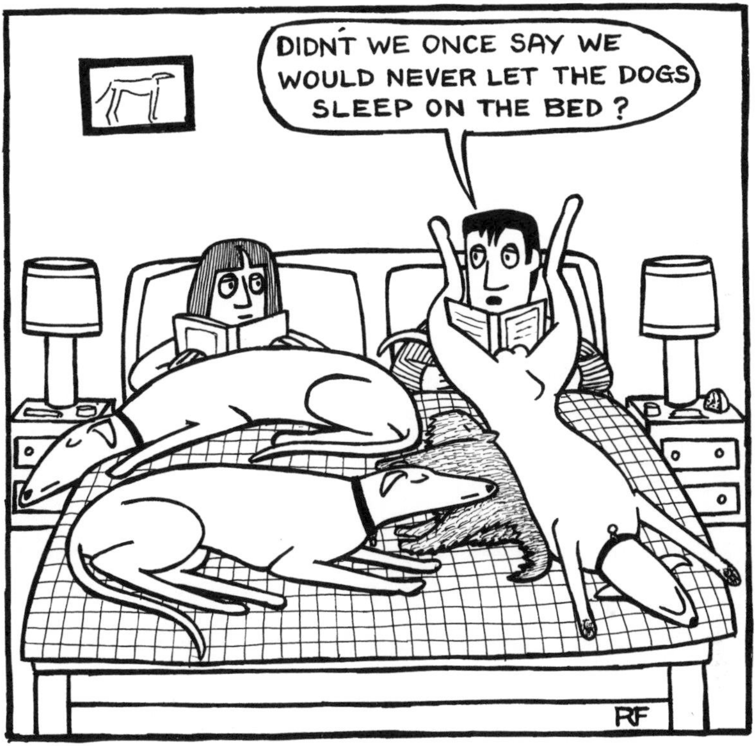
DIDN'T WE ONCE SAY WE WOULD NEVER LET THE DOGS SLEEP ON THE BED ?
RF

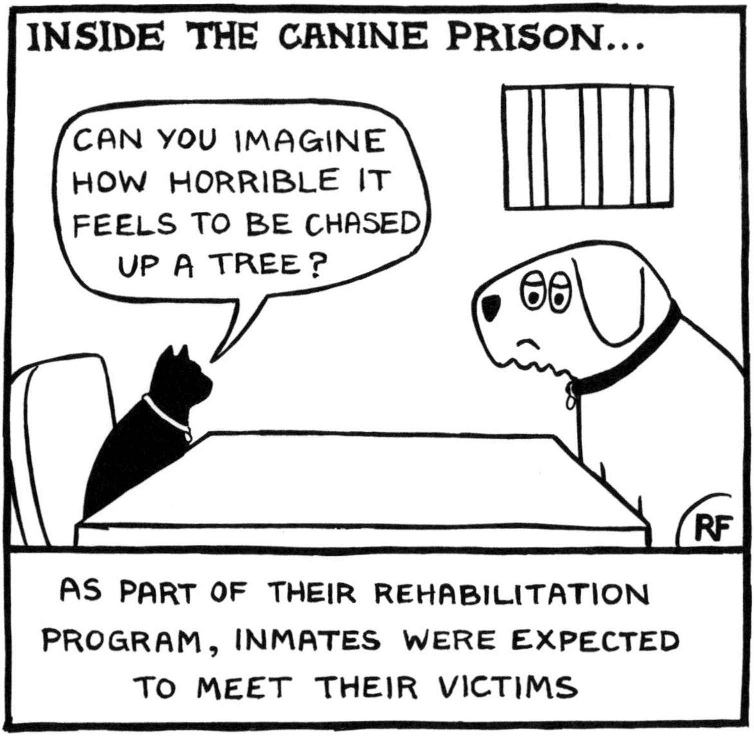
INSIDE THE CANINE PRISON...
CAN YOU IMAGINE HOW HORRIBLE IT FEELS TO BE CHASED UP A TREE?
RF
AS PART OF THEIR REHABILITATION PROGRAM, INMATES WERE EXPECTED TO MEET THEIR VICTIMS

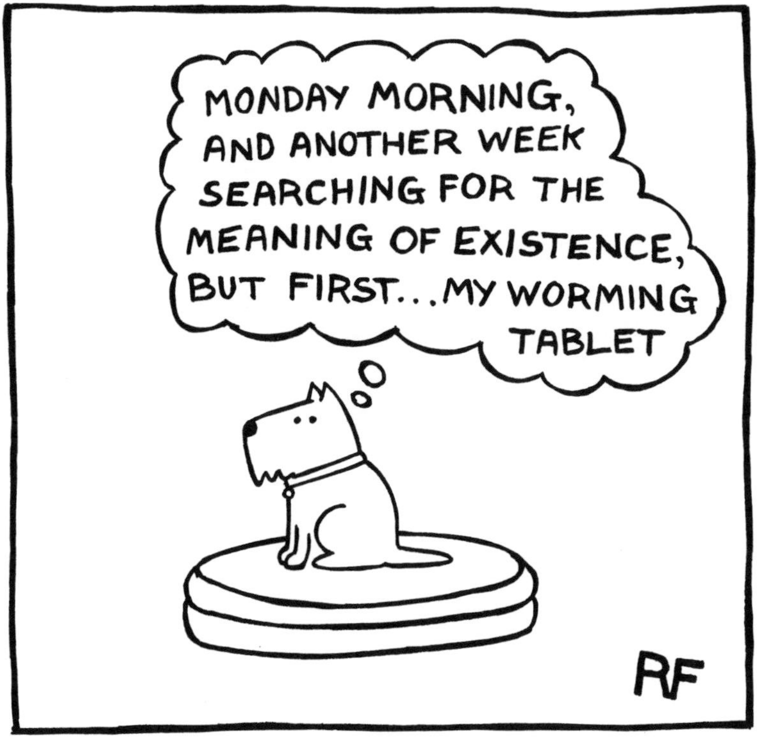
MONDAY MORNING, AND ANOTHER WEEK SEARCHING FOR THE MEANING OF EXISTENCE, BUT FIRST...MY WORMING TABLET
RF

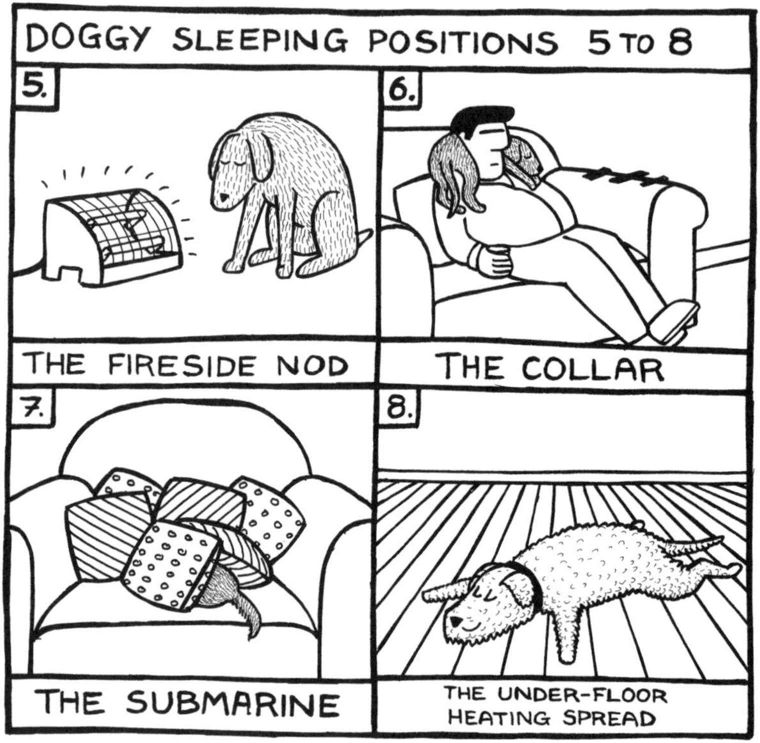
DOGGY SLEEPING POSITIONS 5 TO 8
5.
THE FIRESIDE NOD
6.
THE COLLAR
7.
THE SUBMARINE
8.
THE UNDER-FLOOR HEATING SPREAD

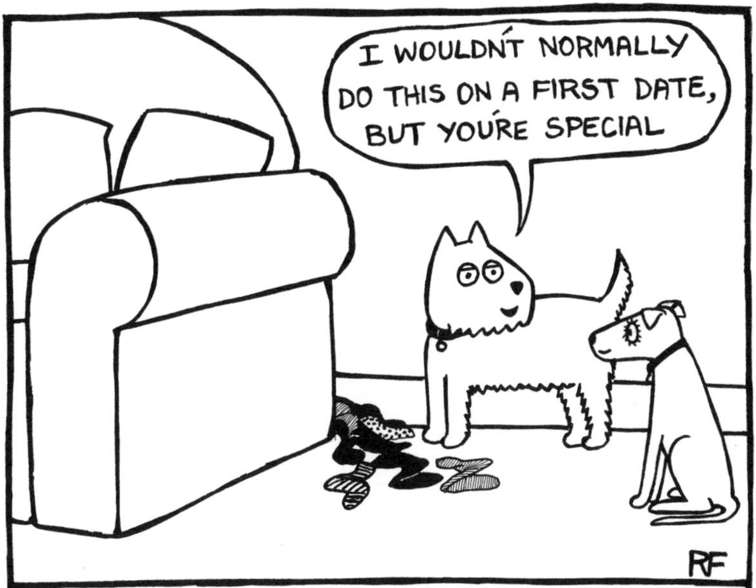
I WOULDN'T NORMALLY DO THIS ON A FIRST DATE, BUT YOU'RE SPECIAL
RF

STANLEY SHOWS HIS NEW FRIEND, EMMA, HIS SECRET STOLEN SOCK COLLECTION

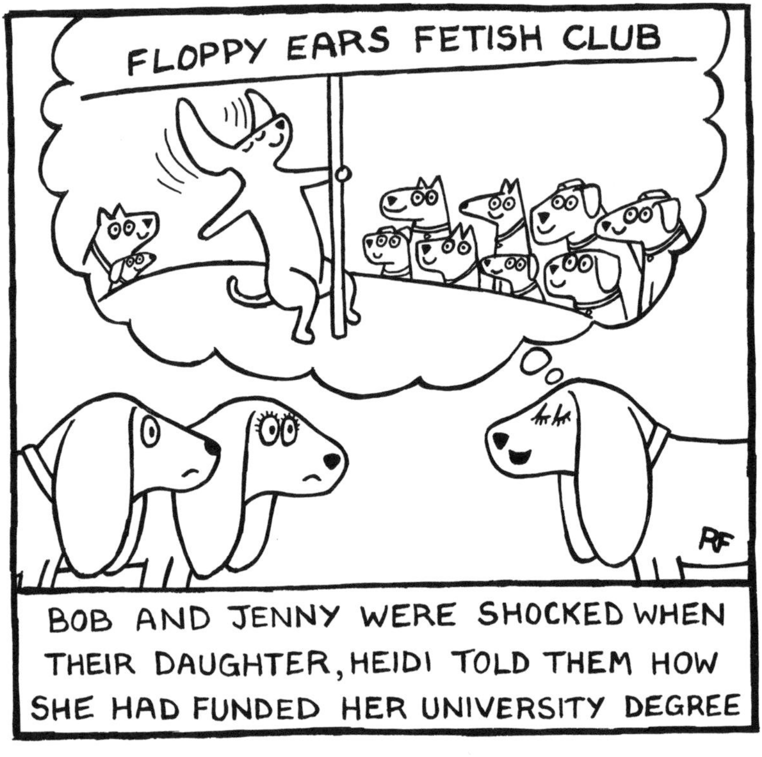
FLOPPY EARS FETISH CLUB
RF
BOB AND JENNY WERE SHOCKED WHEN THEIR DAUGHTER, HEIDI TOLD THEM HOW SHE HAD FUNDED HER UNIVERSITY DEGREE

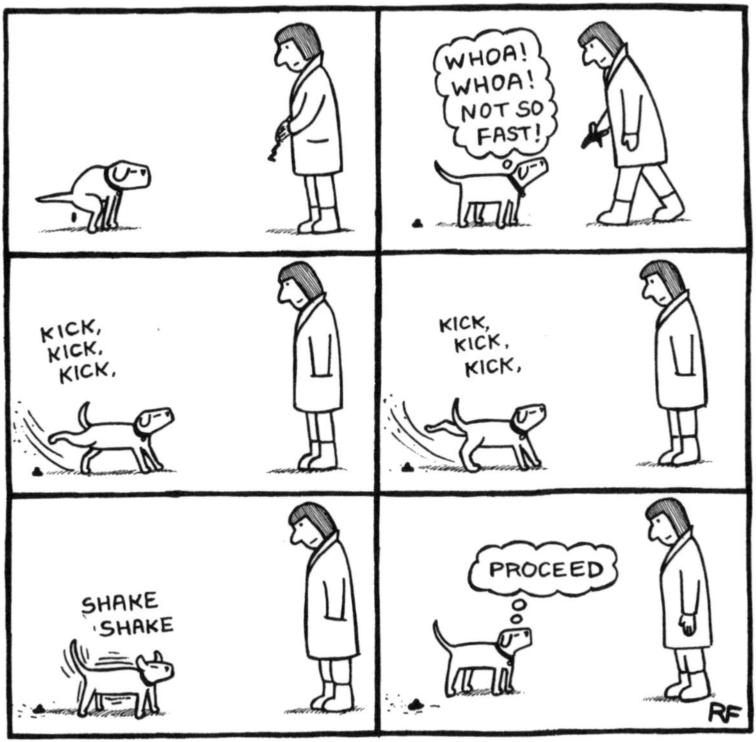
WHOA! WHOA! NOT SO FAST!
KICK, KICK, KICK,
KICK, KICK, KICK,
SHAKE SHAKE
PROCEED
RF

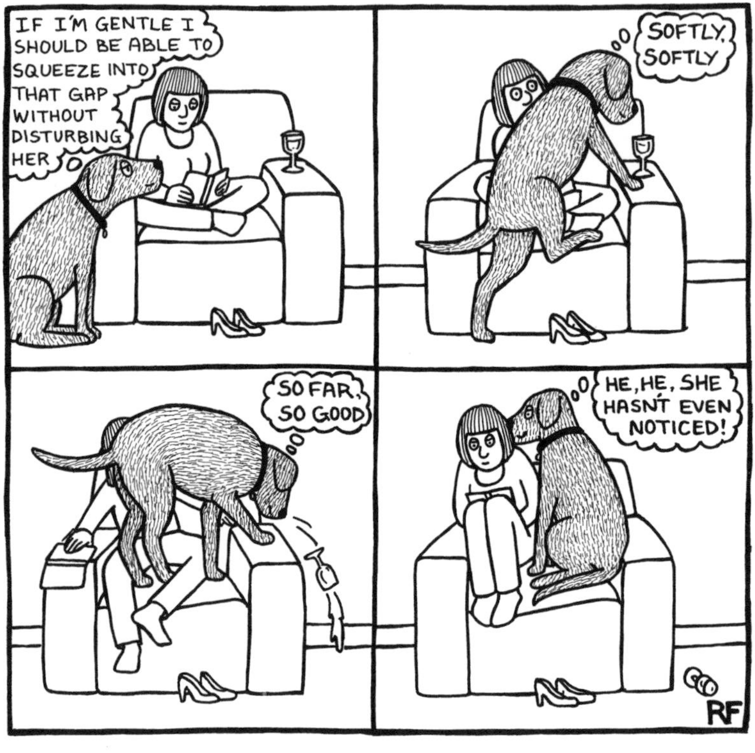
IF I'M GENTLE I SHOULD BE ABLE TO SQUEEZE INTO THAT GAP WITHOUT DISTURBING HER
SOFTLY, SOFTLY
SO FAR, SO GOOD
HE, HE, SHE HASN'T EVEN NOTICED!
RF

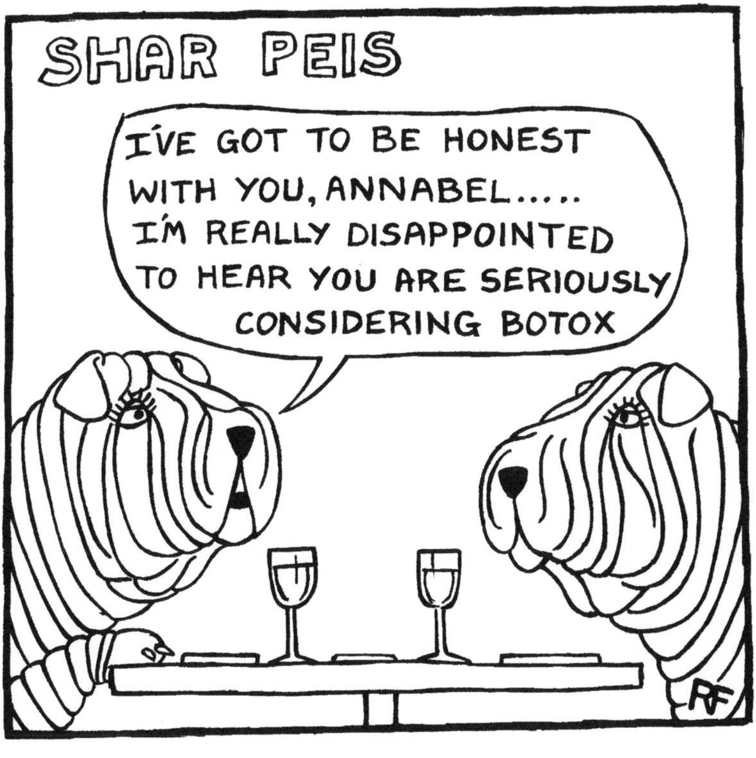
SHAR PEIS
I'VE GOT TO BE HONEST WITH YOU, ANNABEL..... I'M REALLY DISAPPOINTED TO HEAR YOU ARE SERIOUSLY CONSIDERING BOTOX
RF

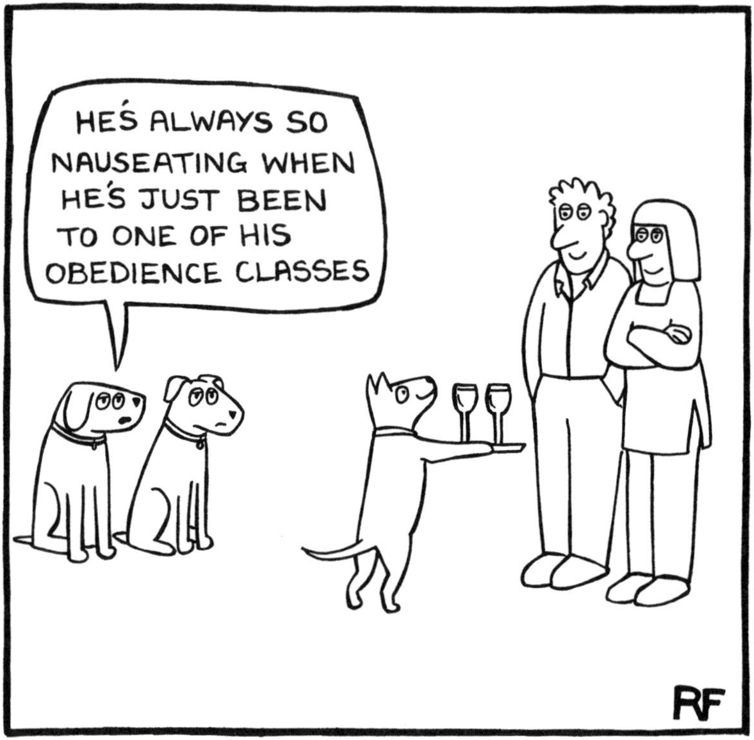
HE'S ALWAYS SO NAUSEATING WHEN HE'S JUST BEEN TO ONE OF HIS OBEDIENCE CLASSES
RF

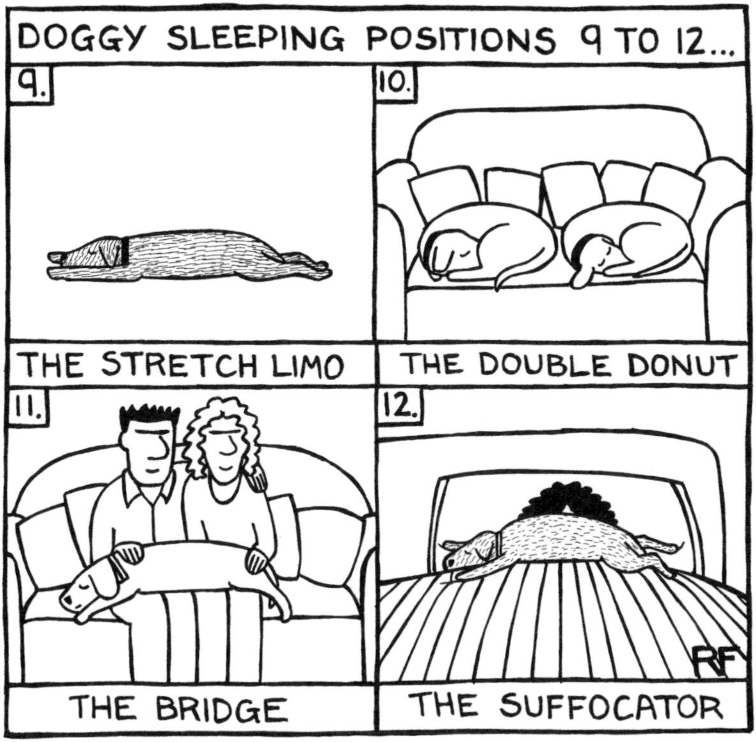
DOGGY SLEEPING POSITIONS 9 TO 12...
9.
THE STRETCH LIMO
10.
THE DOUBLE DONUT
11.
THE BRIDGE
12.
THE SUFFOCATOR
RF

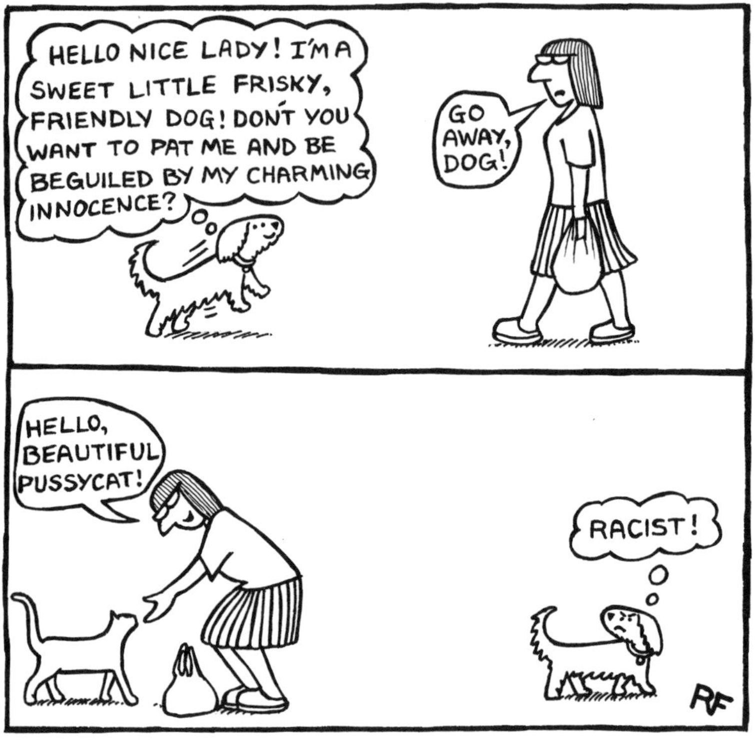
HELLO NICE LADY! I'M A SWEET LITTLE FRISKY, FRIENDLY DOG! DON'T YOU WANT TO PAT ME AND BE BEGUILED BY MY CHARMING INNOCENCE?
GO AWAY, DOG!
HELLO, BEAUTIFUL PUSSYCAT!
RACIST!
RF

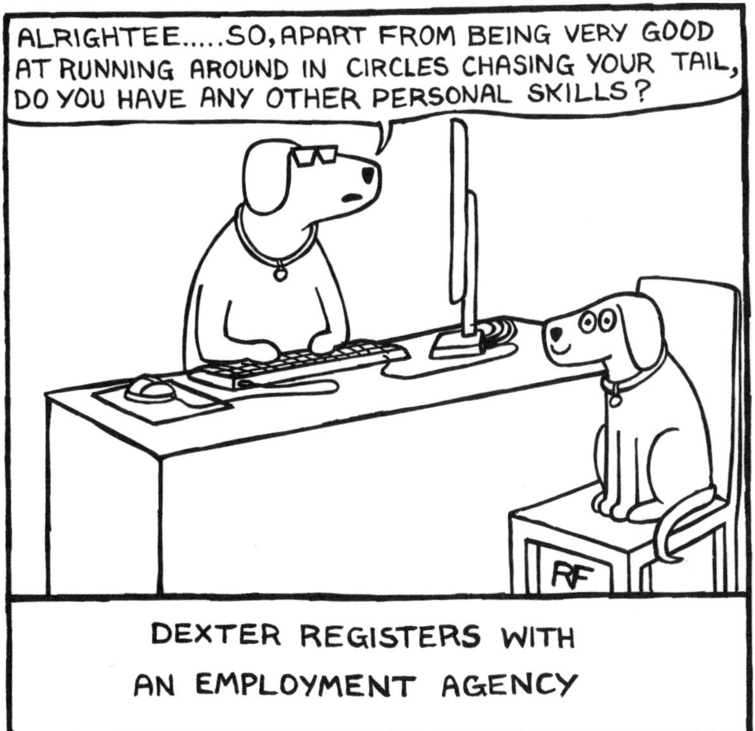
ALRIGHTEE.....SO, APART FROM BEING VERY GOOD AT RUNNING AROUND IN CIRCLES CHASING YOUR TAIL, DO YOU HAVE ANY OTHER PERSONAL SKILLS?
RF
DEXTER REGISTERS WITH AN EMPLOYMENT AGENCY

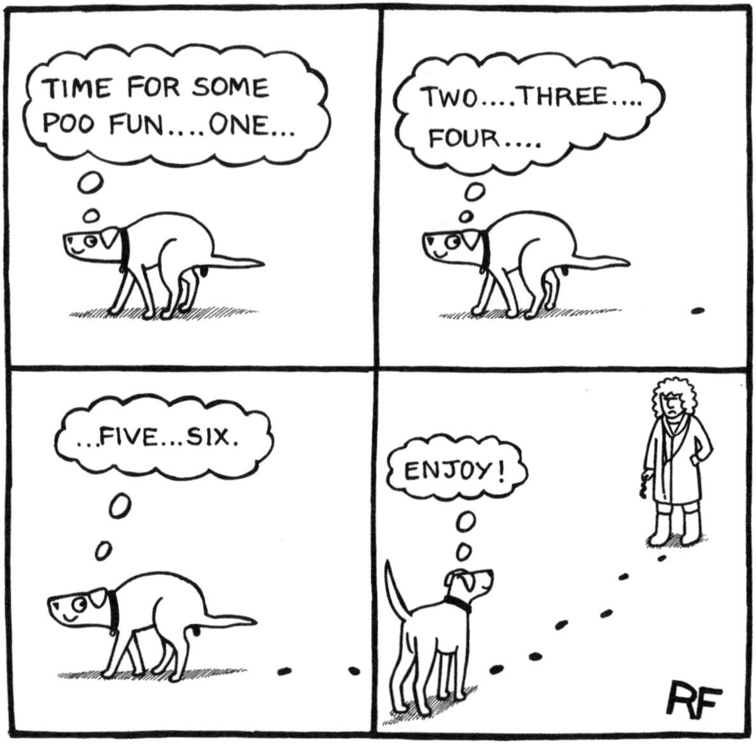
TIME FOR SOME POO FUN....ONE...
TWO....THREE....
FOUR....
...FIVE...SIX.
ENJOY!
RF

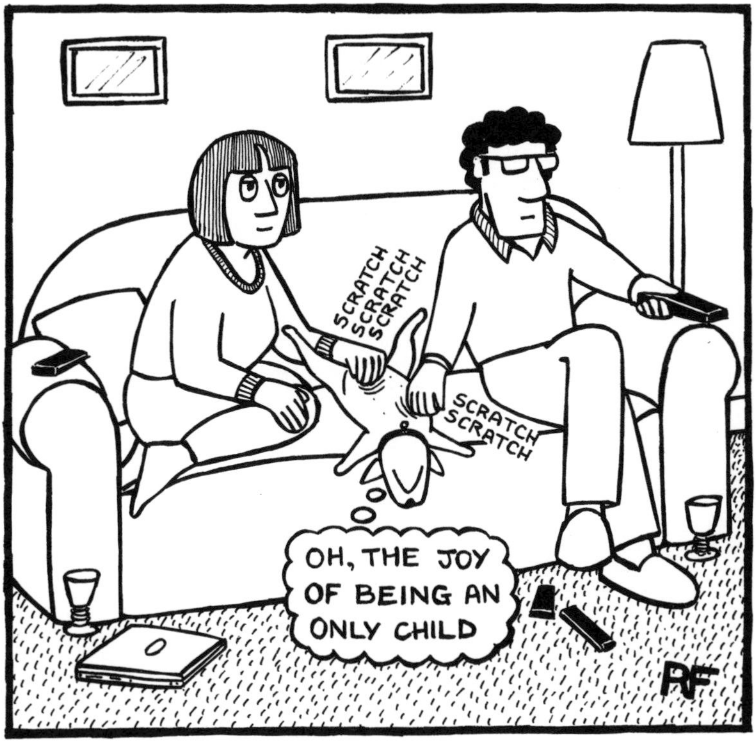
SCRATCH SCRATCH SCRATCH
SCRATCH SCRATCH
OH, THE JOY OF BEING AN ONLY CHILD
RF

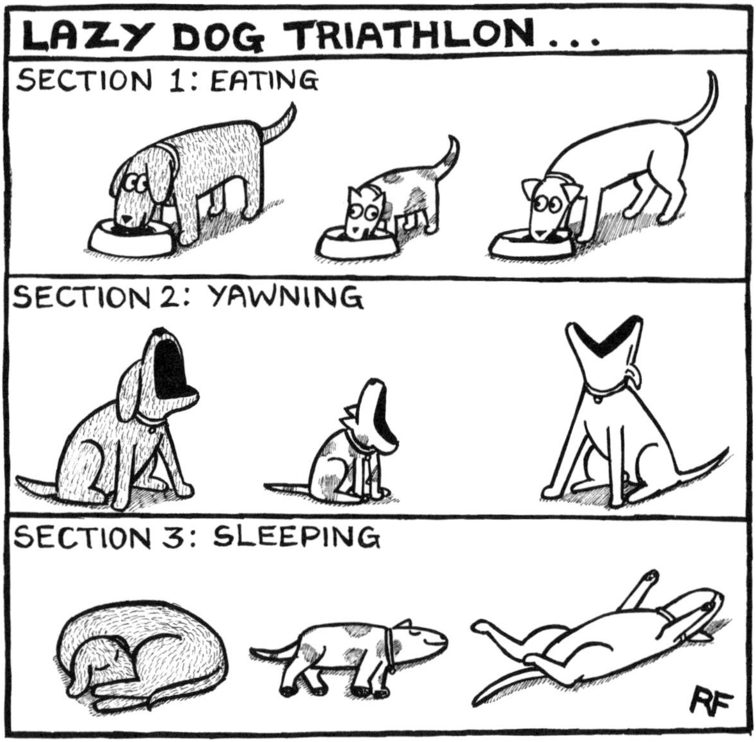
LAZY DOG TRIATHLON ...
SECTION 1: EATING
SECTION 2: YAWNING
SECTION 3: SLEEPING
RF

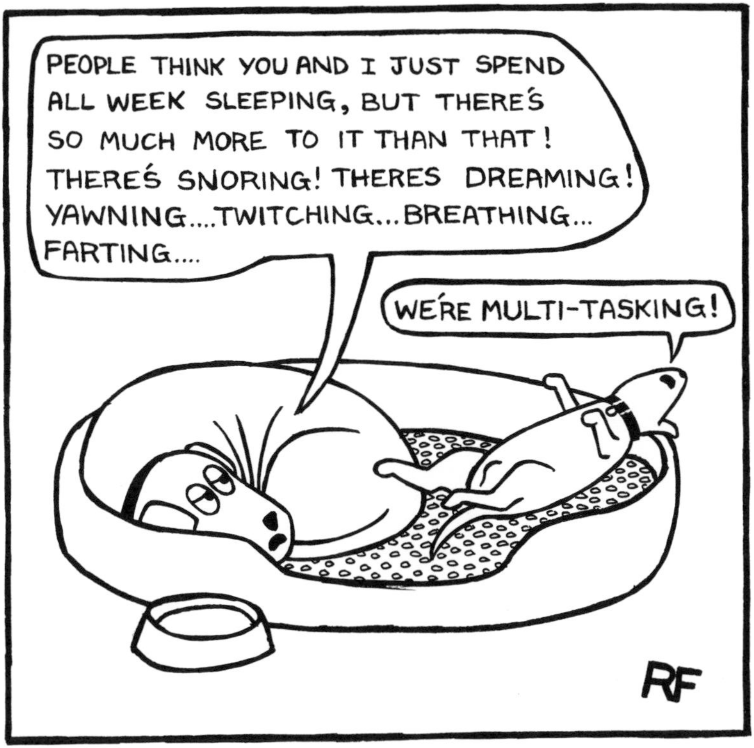
PEOPLE THINK YOU AND I JUST SPEND ALL WEEK SLEEPING, BUT THERE'S SO MUCH MORE TO IT THAN THAT! THERE'S SNORING! THERES DREAMING! YAWNING....TWITCHING...BREATHING... FARTING....
WE'RE MULTI-TASKING!
RF

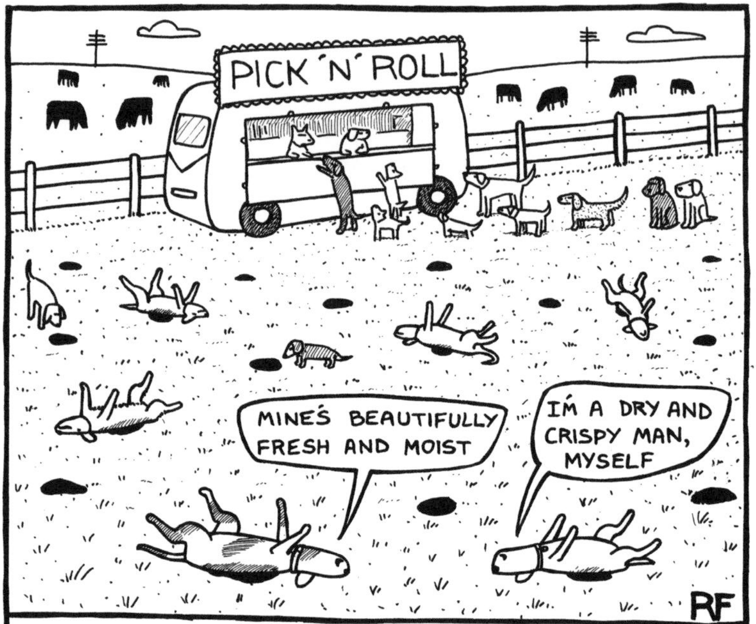
PICK 'N' ROLL
MINE'S BEAUTIFULLY FRESH AND MOIST
I'M A DRY AND CRISPY MAN, MYSELF
RF

AT THE COW PAT PICK'N'ROLL FARM

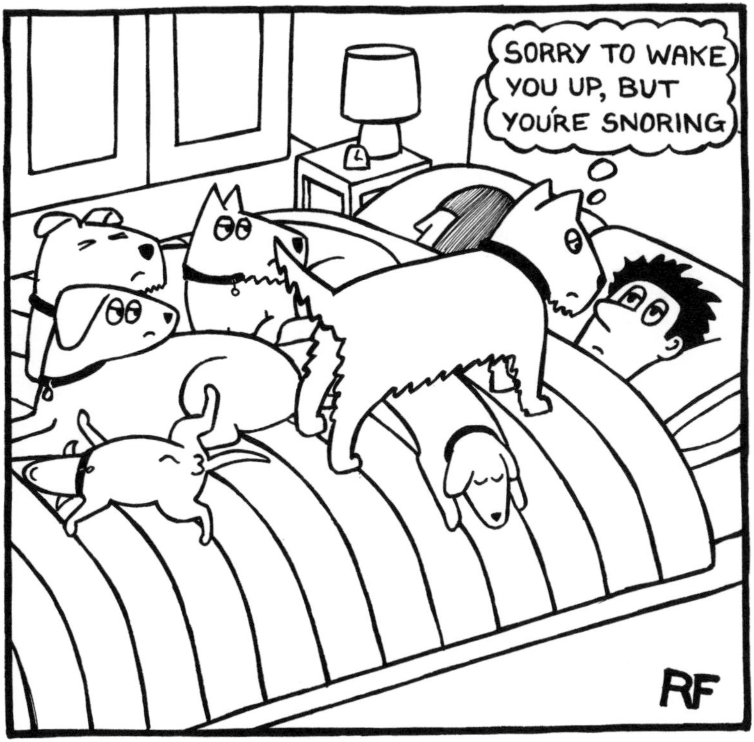
SORRY TO WAKE YOU UP, BUT YOU'RE SNORING
RF

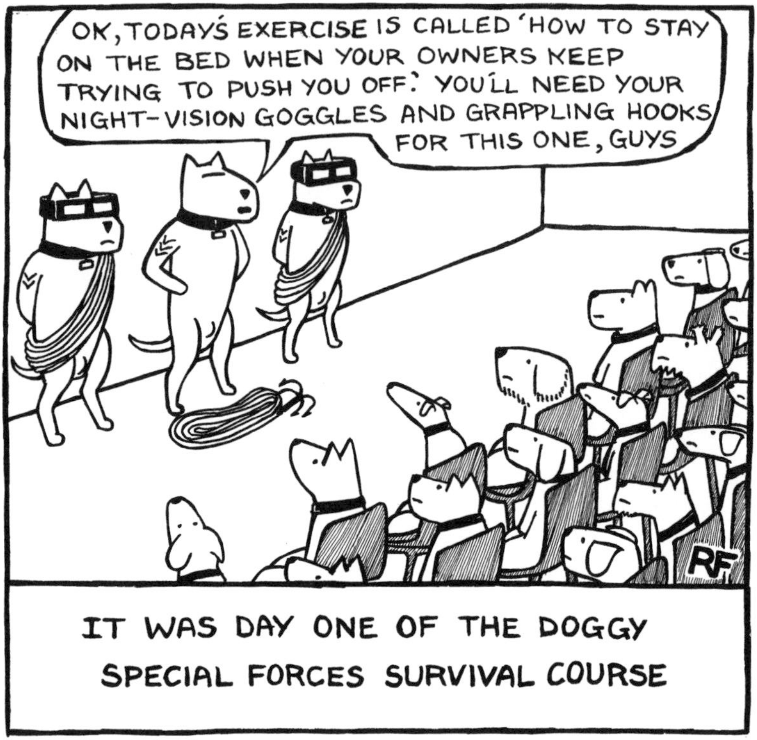
OK, TODAY'S EXERCISE IS CALLED 'HOW TO STAY ON THE BED WHEN YOUR OWNERS KEEP TRYING TO PUSH YOU OFF.' YOU'LL NEED YOUR NIGHT-VISION GOGGLES AND GRAPPLING HOOKS FOR THIS ONE, GUYS
RF
IT WAS DAY ONE OF THE DOGGY SPECIAL FORCES SURVIVAL COURSE

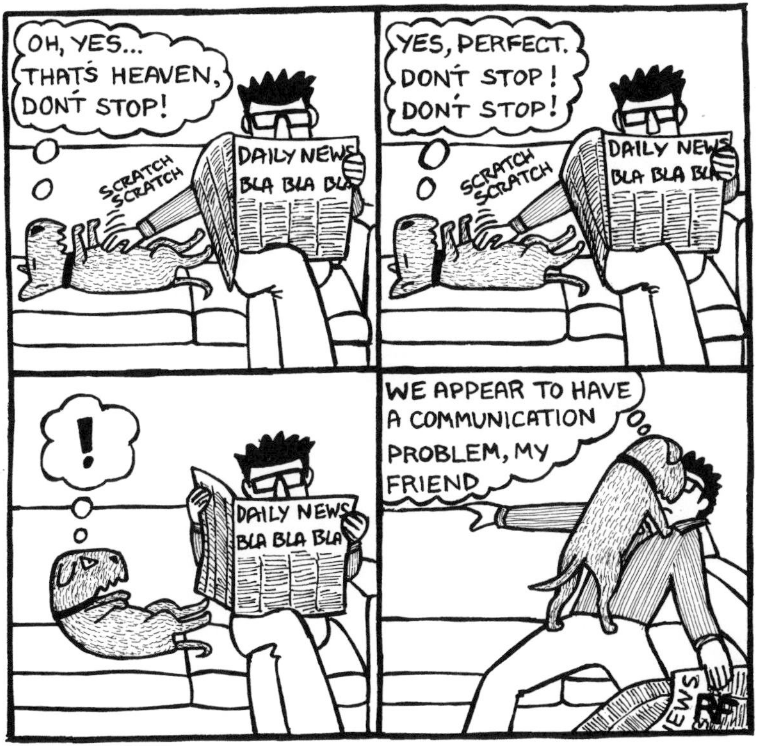
OH, YES... THAT'S HEAVEN, DON'T STOP!
SCRATCH SCRATCH
DAILY NEWS
BLA BLA BLA
YES, PERFECT. DON'T STOP! DON'T STOP!
SCRATCH SCRATCH
DAILY NEWS
BLA BLA BLA
!
DAILY NEWS
BLA BLA BLA
WE APPEAR TO HAVE A COMMUNICATION PROBLEM, MY FRIEND
NEWS

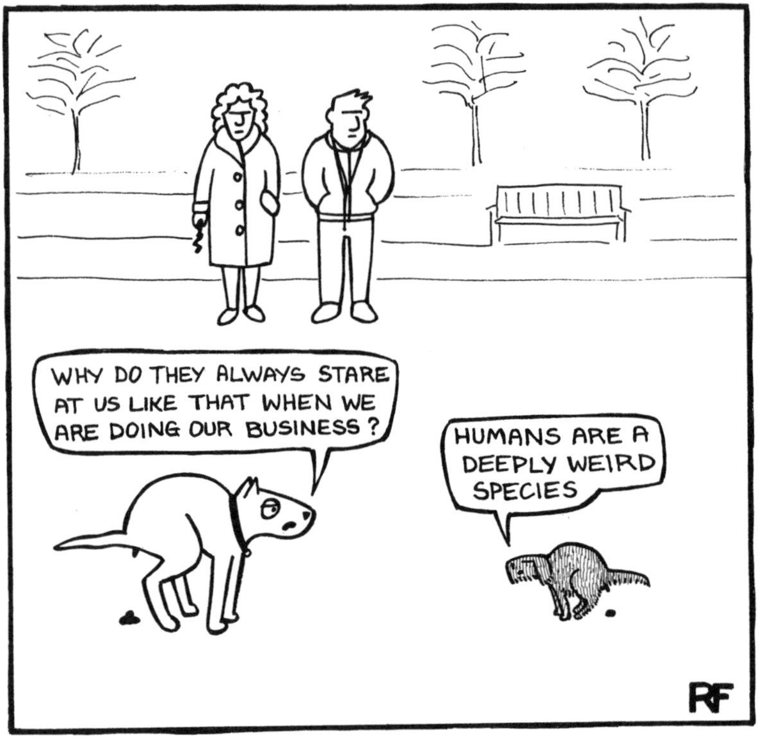
WHY DO THEY ALWAYS STARE AT US LIKE THAT WHEN WE ARE DOING OUR BUSINESS?
HUMANS ARE A DEEPLY WEIRD SPECIES
RF

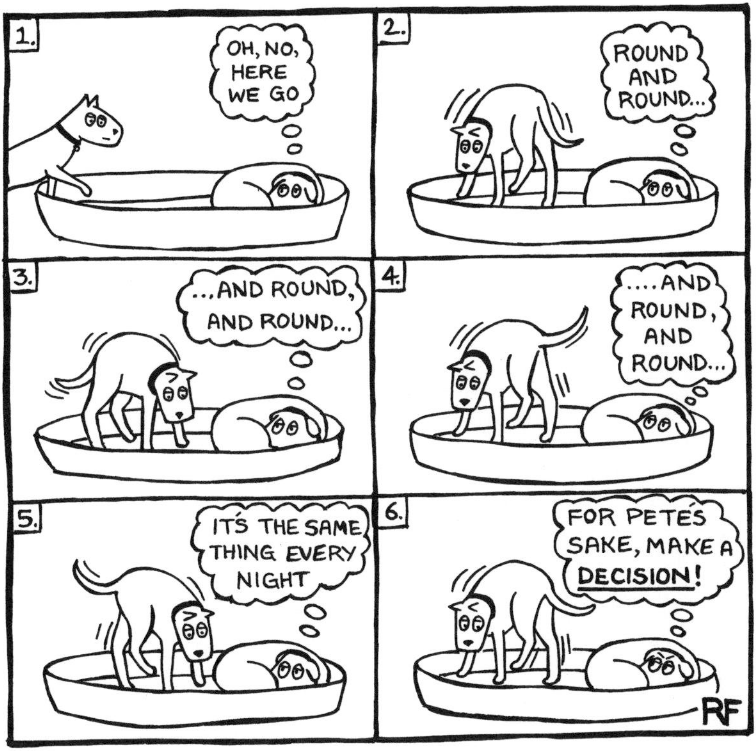
1.
OH, NO, HERE WE GO
2.
ROUND AND ROUND...
3.
...AND ROUND, AND ROUND...
4.
....AND ROUND, AND ROUND...
5.
IT'S THE SAME THING EVERY NIGHT
6.
FOR PETE'S SAKE, MAKE A DECISION!
RF

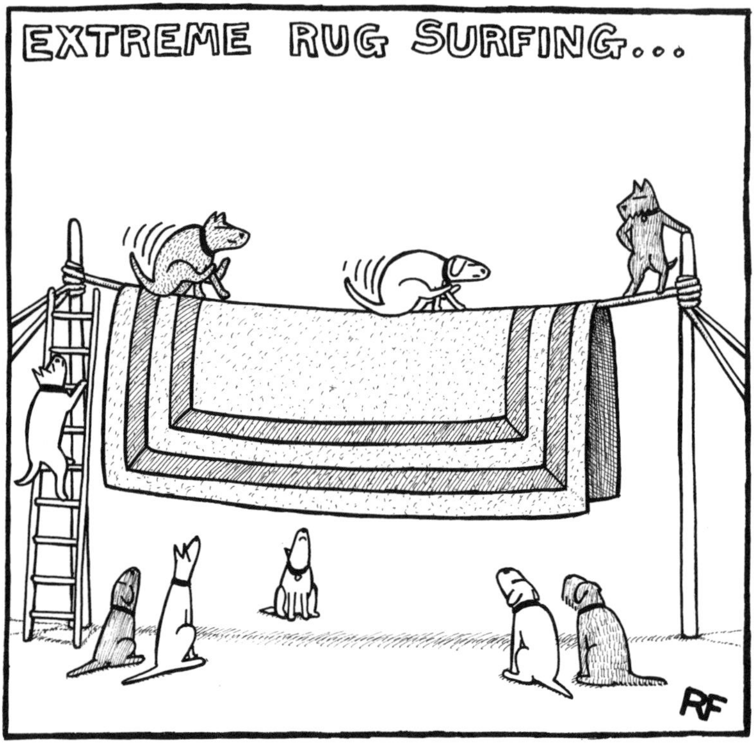
EXTREME RUG SURFING...
RF

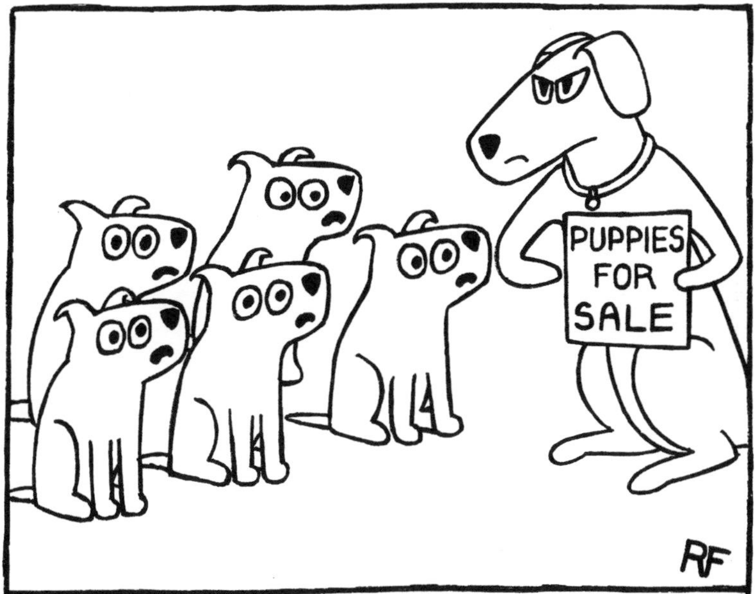
PUPPIES
FOR
SALE
RF

WHENEVER THE KIDS GOT OUT OF HAND POPPY WOULD THREATEN THEM WITH HER FAVOURITE SIGN

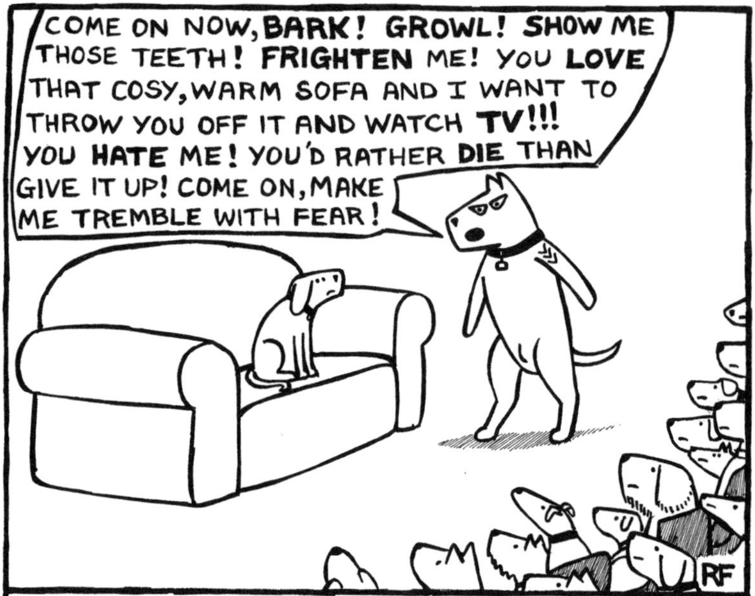
COME ON NOW, BARK! GROWL! SHOW ME THOSE TEETH! FRIGHTEN ME! YOU LOVE THAT COSY, WARM SOFA AND I WANT TO THROW YOU OFF IT AND WATCH TV!!! YOU HATE ME! YOU'D RATHER DIE THAN GIVE IT UP! COME ON, MAKE ME TREMBLE WITH FEAR!
RF

IT WAS THE SECOND DAY OF THE DOGGY SPECIAL FORCES SURVIVAL COURSE AND EXERCISE 2: SOFA OCCUPATION

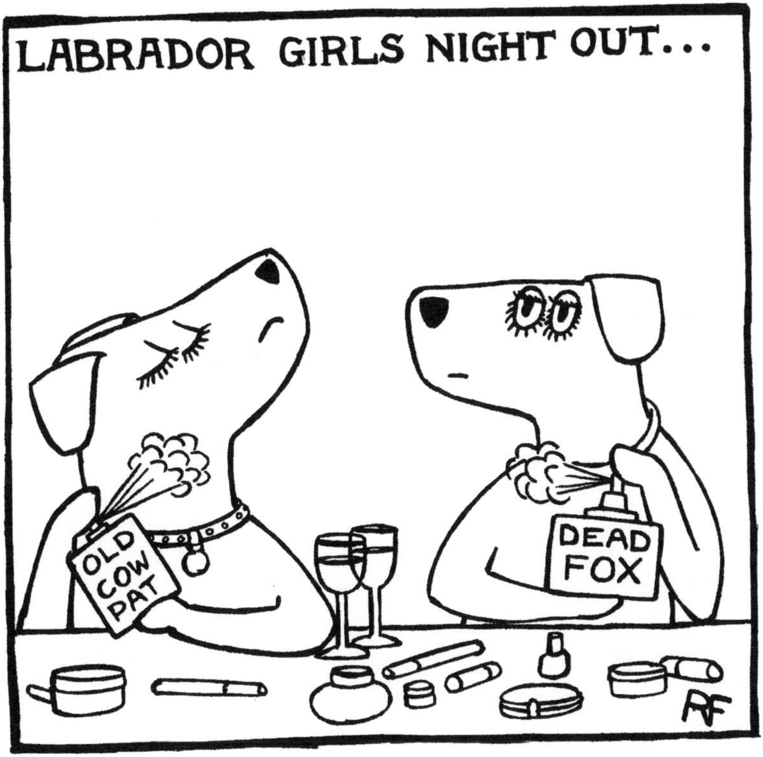
LABRADOR GIRLS NIGHT OUT...
OLD COW PAT
DEAD FOX
RF

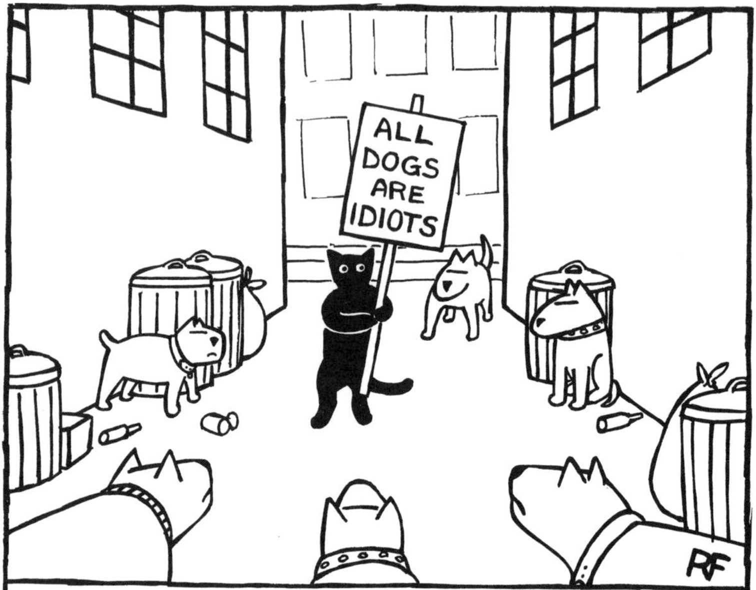
ALL DOGS ARE IDIOTS

HARVEY MADE THE MISTAKE OF TAKING A SHORT-CUT HOME FROM THE ANTI-DOG DEMO

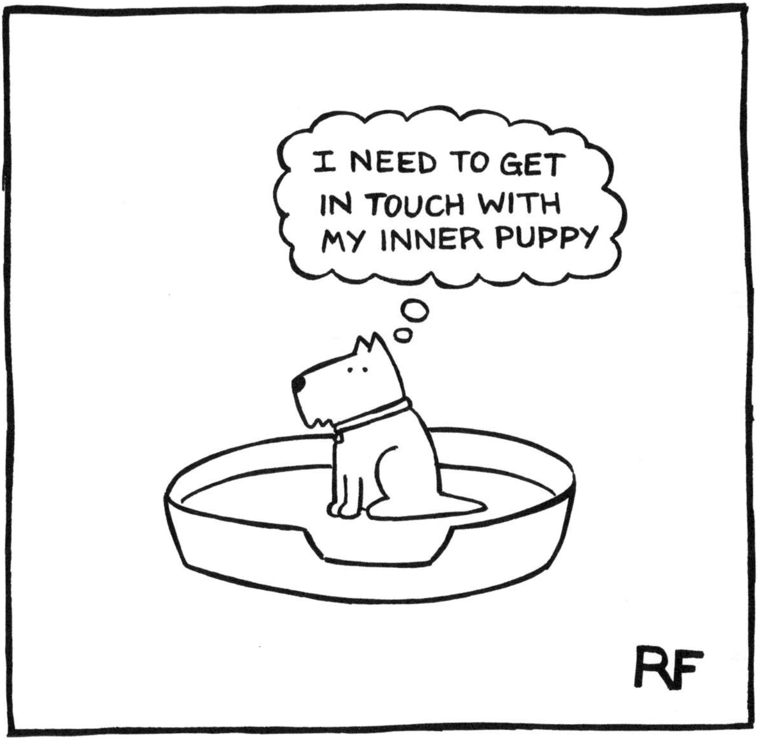
I NEED TO GET IN TOUCH WITH MY INNER PUPPY
RF

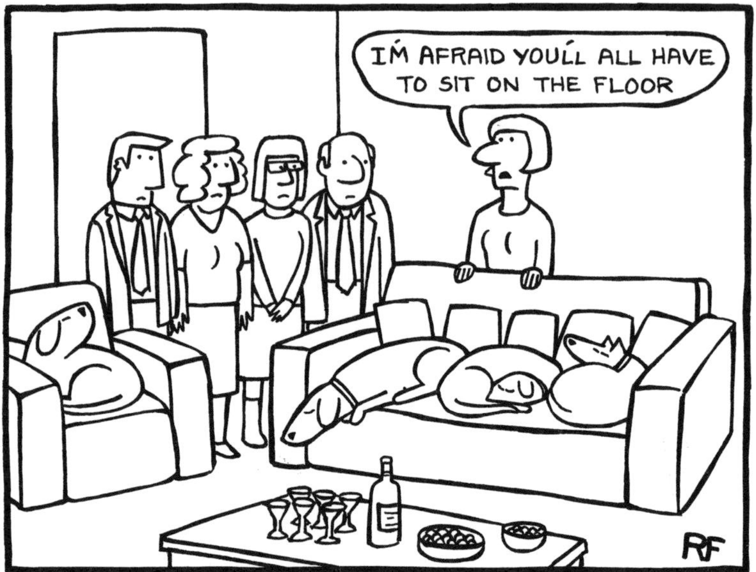
I'M AFRAID YOU'LL ALL HAVE TO SIT ON THE FLOOR
RF

IN BARBARA'S HOUSE THE DOGS CAME FIRST

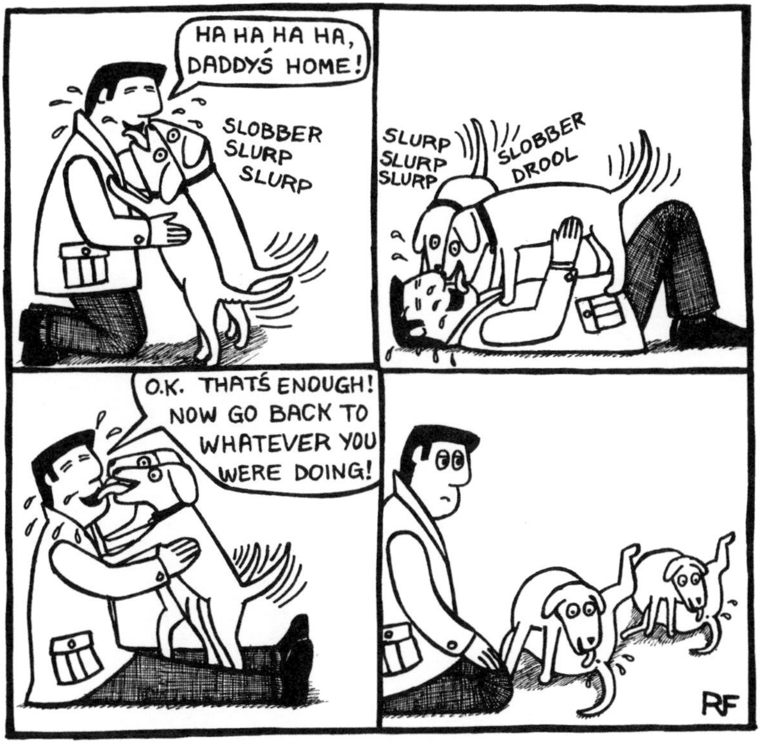
HA HA HA HA, DADDY'S HOME!
SLOBBER SLURP SLURP
SLURP SLURP SLURP
SLOBBER DROOL
O.K. THAT'S ENOUGH! NOW GO BACK TO WHATEVER YOU WERE DOING!
RF

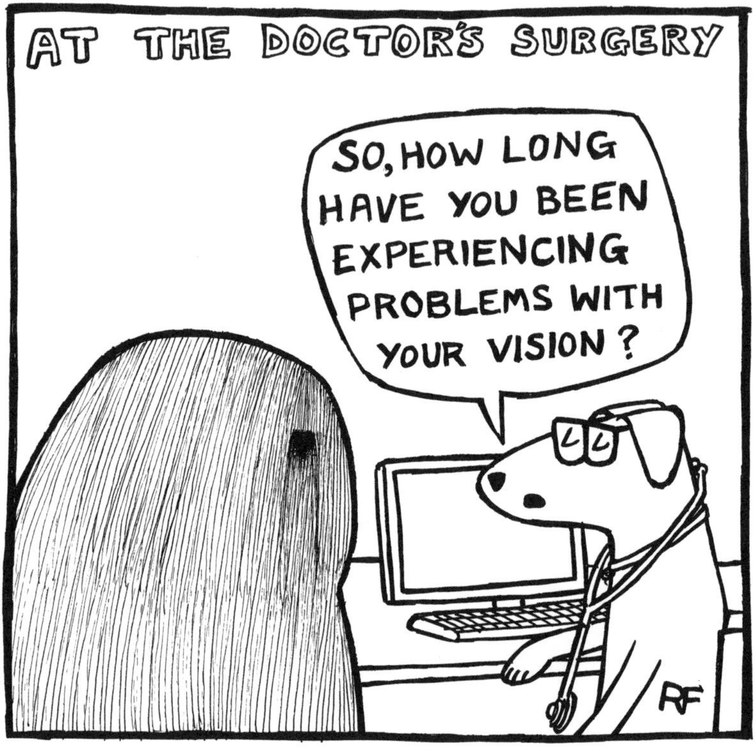
AT THE DOCTOR'S SURGERY
SO, HOW LONG HAVE YOU BEEN EXPERIENCING PROBLEMS WITH YOUR VISION?
RF

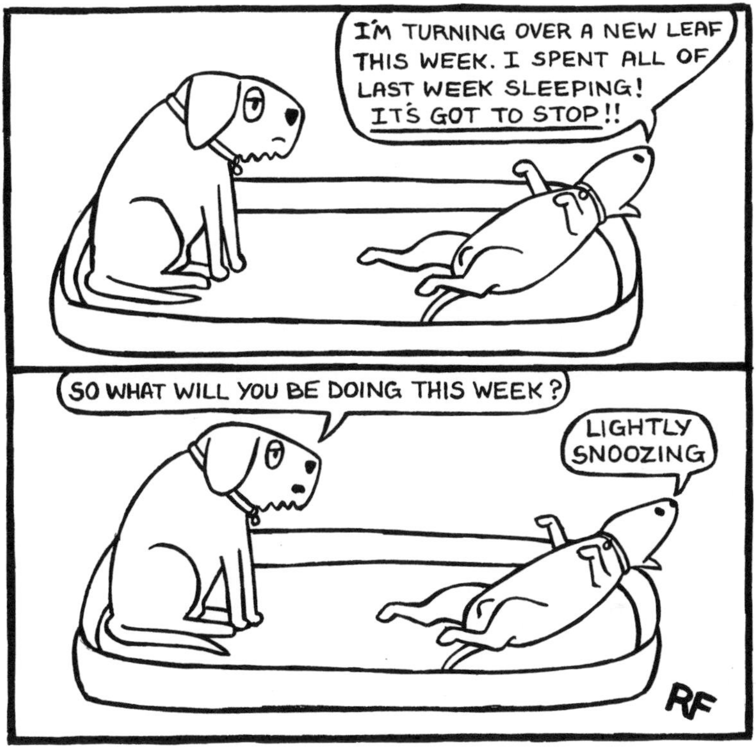
I'M TURNING OVER A NEW LEAF THIS WEEK. I SPENT ALL OF LAST WEEK SLEEPING! IT'S GOT TO STOP!!
SO WHAT WILL YOU BE DOING THIS WEEK?
LIGHTLY SNOOZING
RF

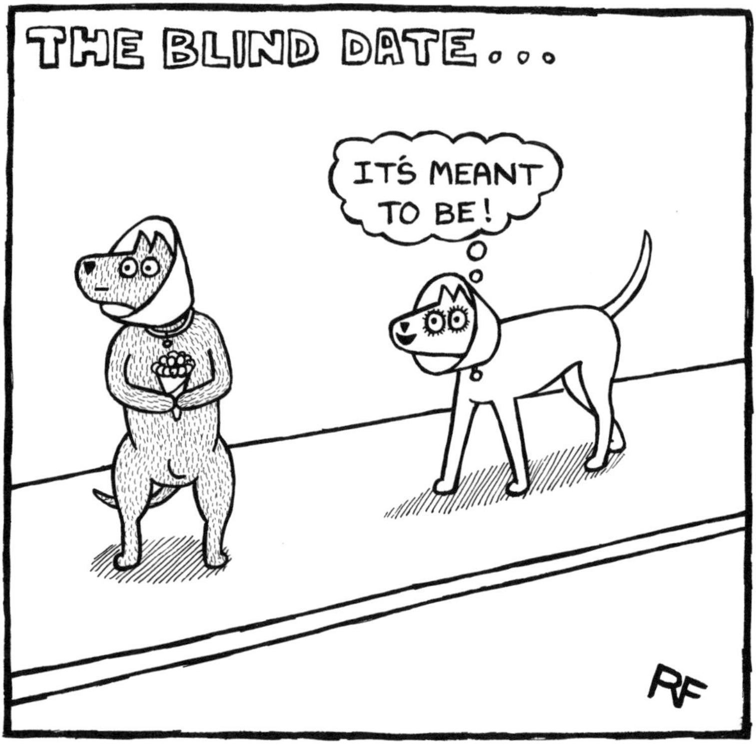
THE BLIND DATE...
IT'S MEANT TO BE!
RF

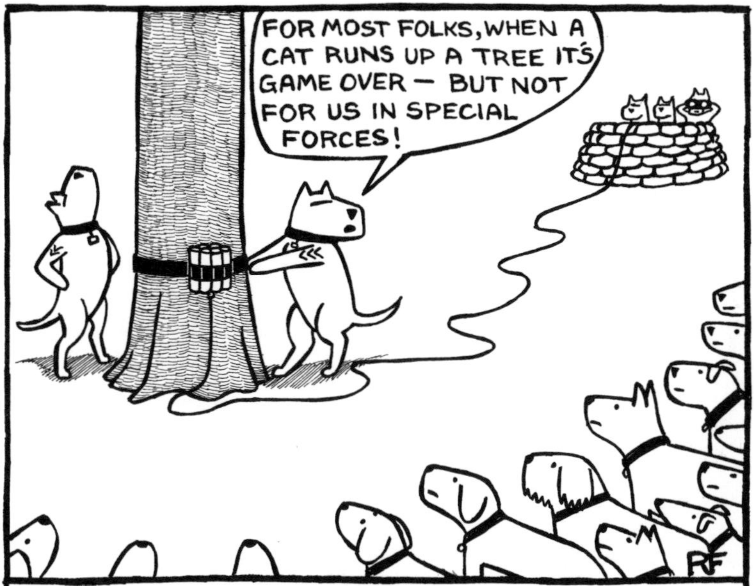
FOR MOST FOLKS, WHEN A CAT RUNS UP A TREE IT'S GAME OVER — BUT NOT FOR US IN SPECIAL FORCES!
RF

EXERCISE NUMBER THREE IN THE DOGGY SURVIVAL COURSE WAS 'PURSUIT OF THE FELINE'

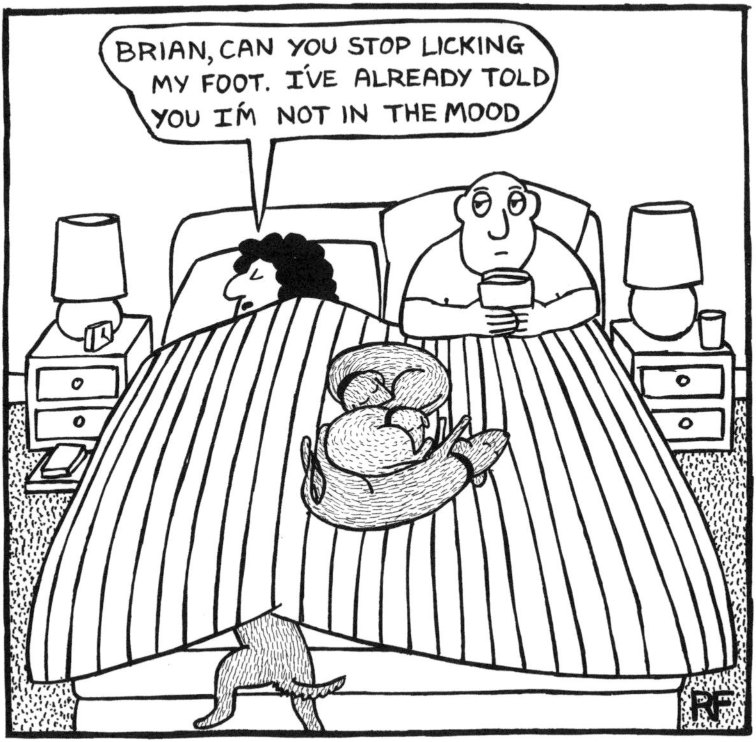
BRIAN, CAN YOU STOP LICKING MY FOOT. I'VE ALREADY TOLD YOU I'M NOT IN THE MOOD
RF

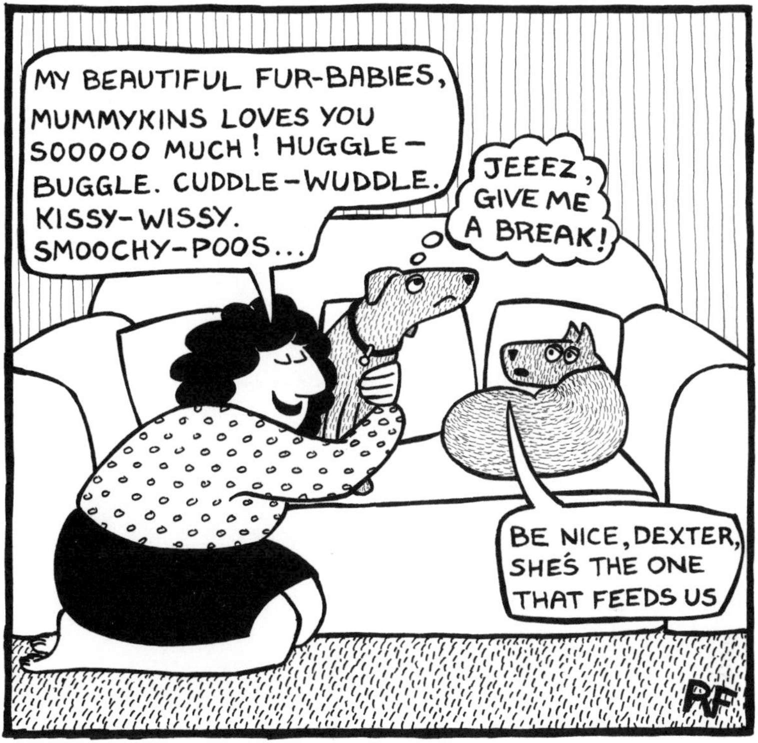
MY BEAUTIFUL FUR-BABIES, MUMMYKINS LOVES YOU SOOOOO MUCH! HUGGLE-BUGGLE. CUDDLE-WUDDLE. KISSY-WISSY. SMOOCHY-POOS...
JEEEZ, GIVE ME A BREAK!
BE NICE, DEXTER, SHE'S THE ONE THAT FEEDS US
RF

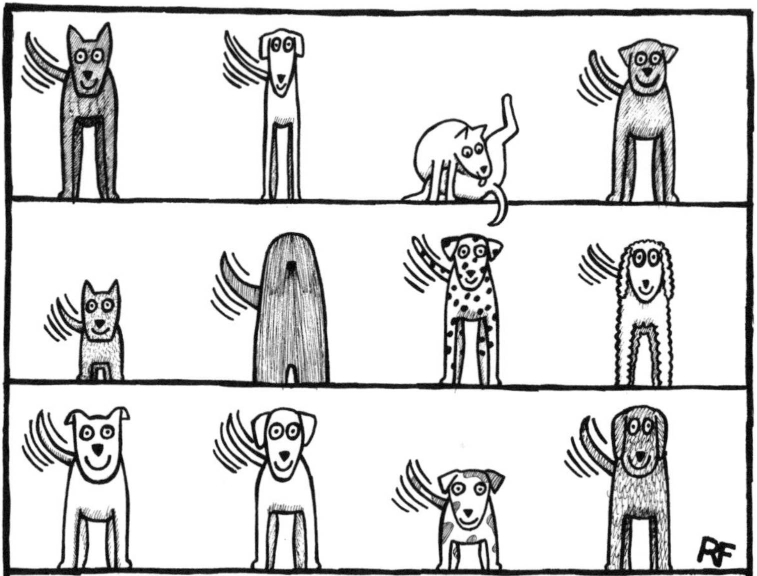
RF

SADLY FOR THE TEAM, COLIN'S DISAPPOINTING PERFORMANCE IN THE SYNCHRONISED TAIL-WAGGING COST THEM A MEDAL

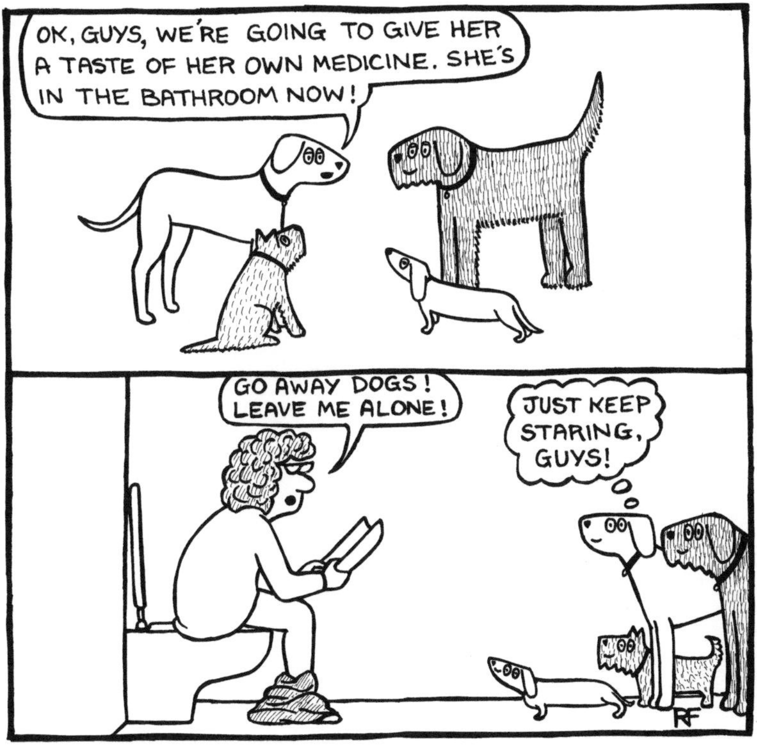
OK, GUYS, WE'RE GOING TO GIVE HER A TASTE OF HER OWN MEDICINE. SHE'S IN THE BATHROOM NOW!
GO AWAY DOGS! LEAVE ME ALONE!
JUST KEEP STARING, GUYS!
RF

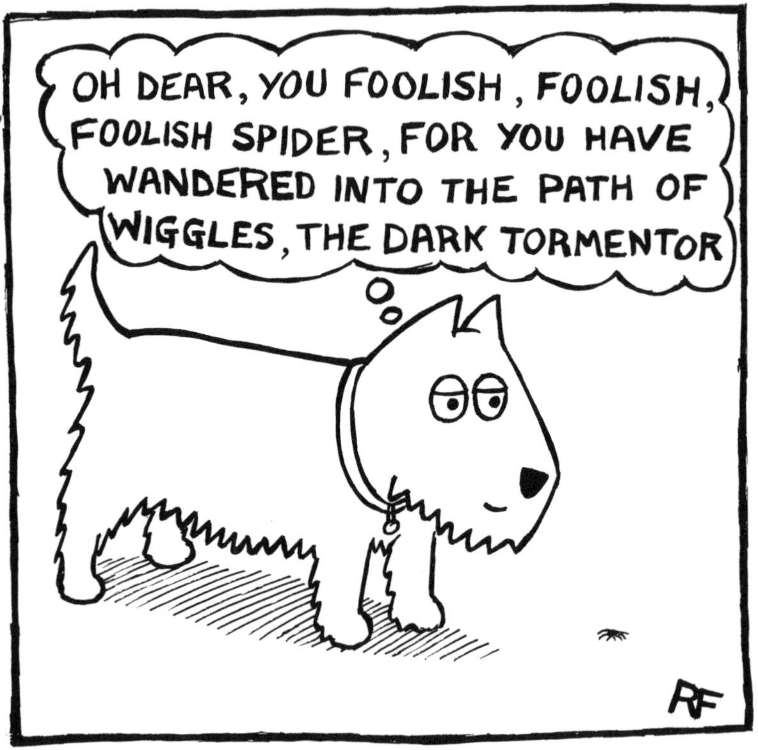
OH DEAR, YOU FOOLISH, FOOLISH, FOOLISH SPIDER, FOR YOU HAVE WANDERED INTO THE PATH OF WIGGLES, THE DARK TORMENTOR
RF

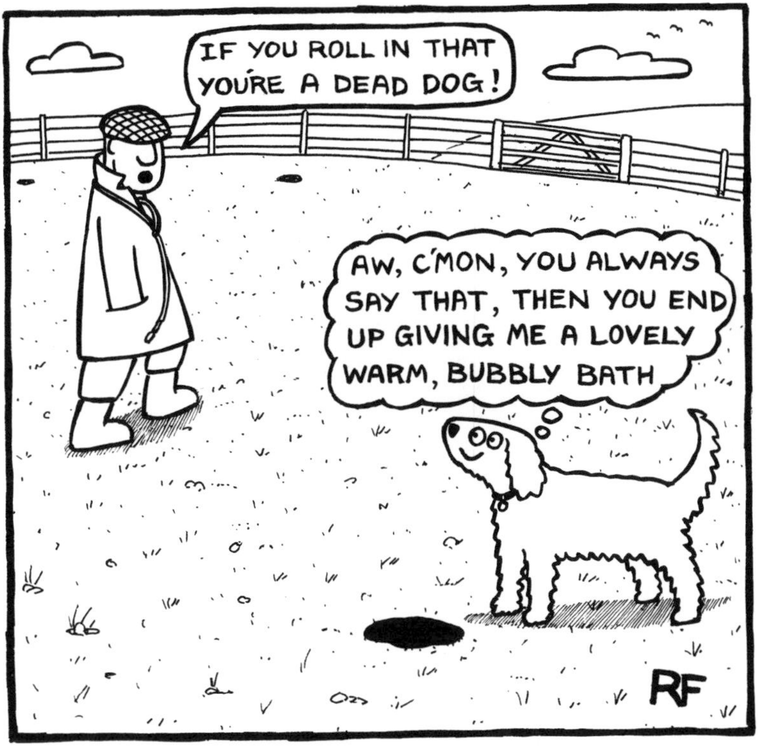
IF YOU ROLL IN THAT YOU'RE A DEAD DOG!
AW, C'MON, YOU ALWAYS SAY THAT, THEN YOU END UP GIVING ME A LOVELY WARM, BUBBLY BATH
RF

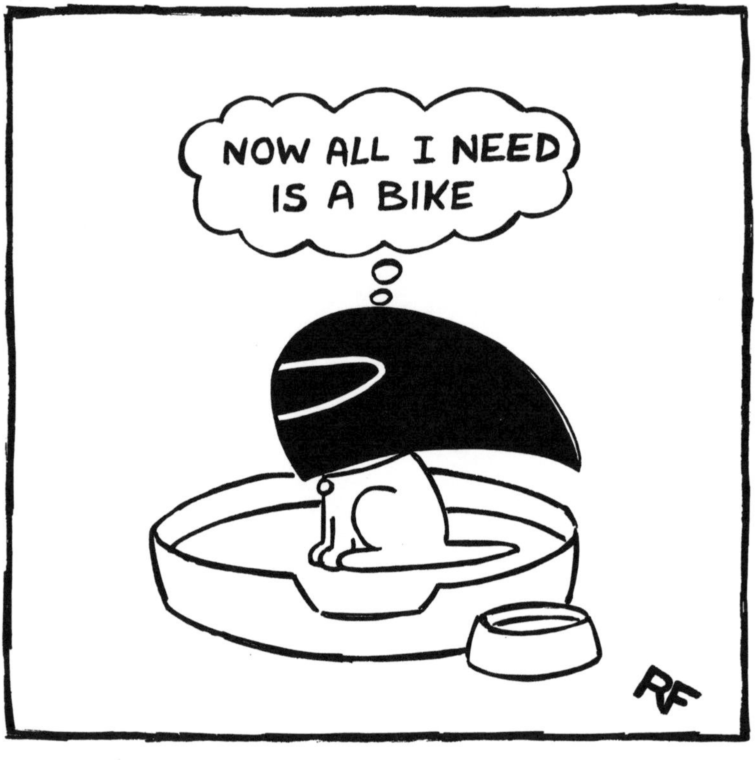
NOW ALL I NEED IS A BIKE
RF

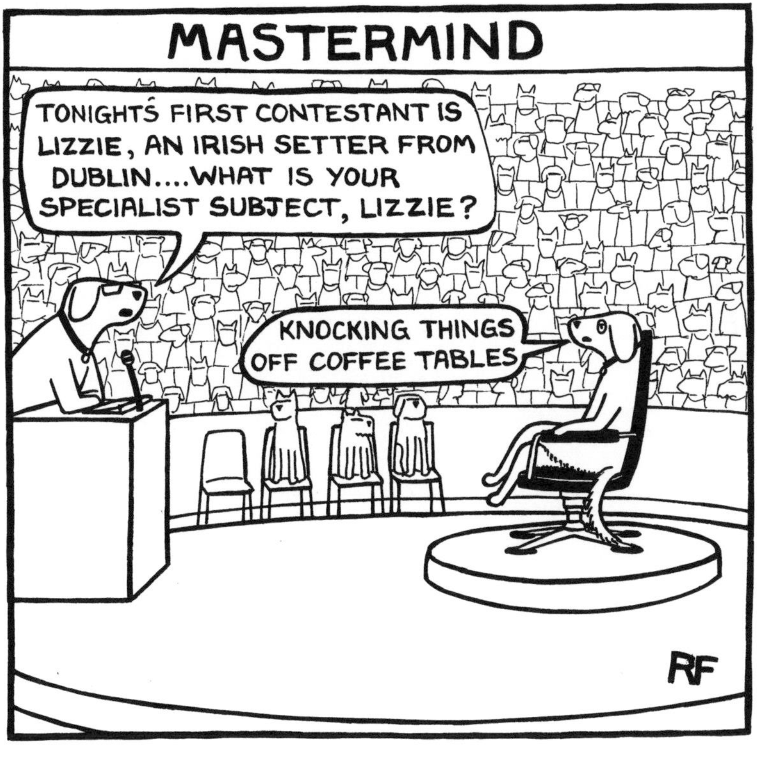
MASTERMIND
TONIGHTS FIRST CONTESTANT IS LIZZIE, AN IRISH SETTER FROM DUBLIN....WHAT IS YOUR SPECIALIST SUBJECT, LIZZIE?
KNOCKING THINGS OFF COFFEE TABLES
RF

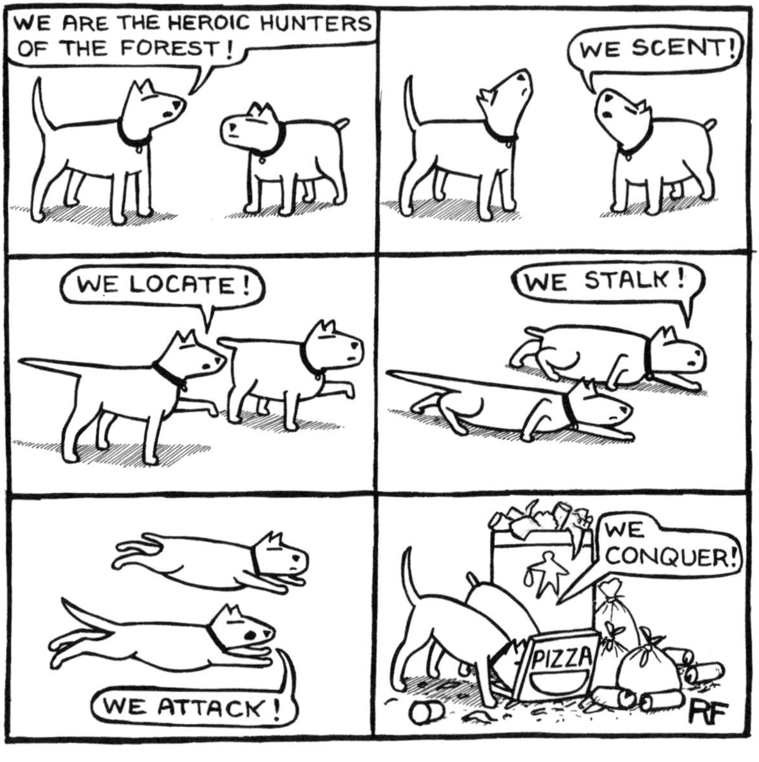
WE ARE THE HEROIC HUNTERS OF THE FOREST!
WE SCENT!
WE LOCATE!
WE STALK!
WE ATTACK!
PIZZA
WE CONQUER!
RF

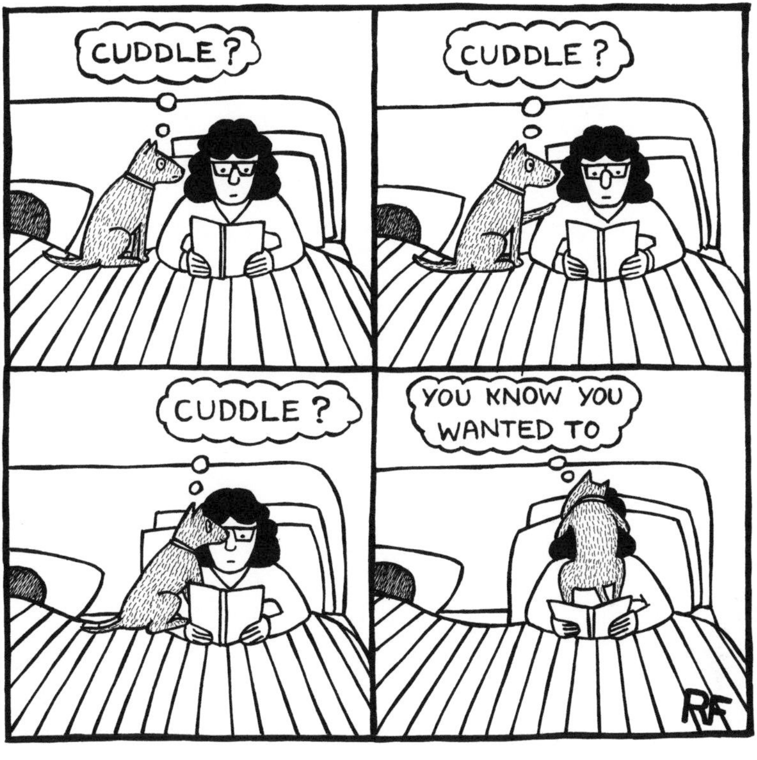
CUDDLE?
CUDDLE?
CUDDLE?
YOU KNOW YOU WANTED TO
RF

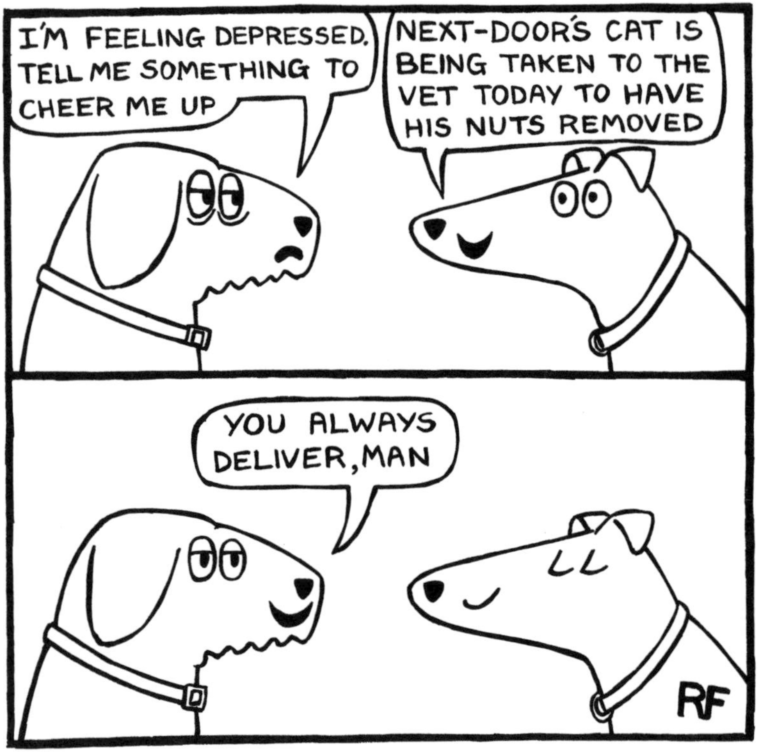
I'M FEELING DEPRESSED. TELL ME SOMETHING TO CHEER ME UP
NEXT-DOOR'S CAT IS BEING TAKEN TO THE VET TODAY TO HAVE HIS NUTS REMOVED
YOU ALWAYS DELIVER, MAN
RF

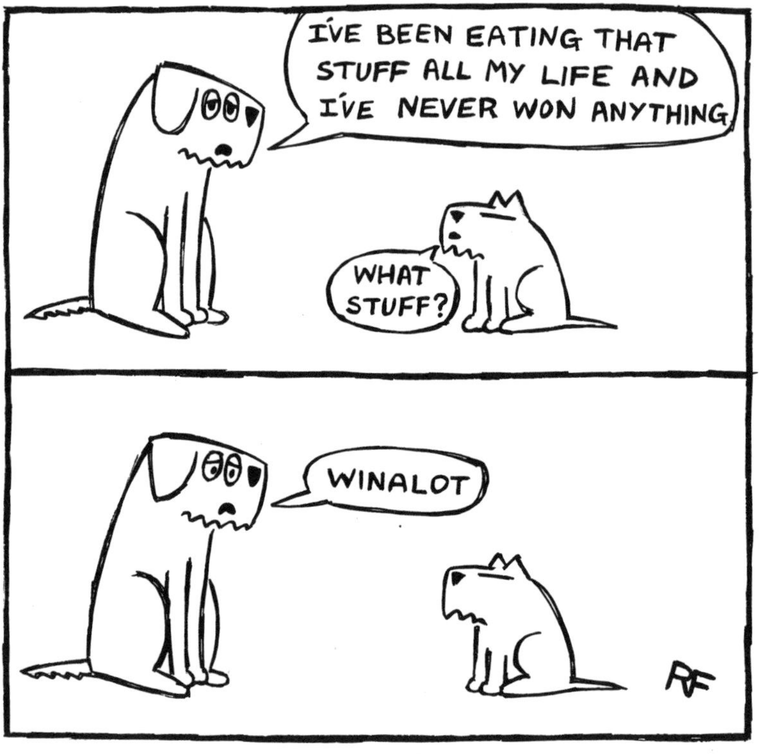
I'VE BEEN EATING THAT STUFF ALL MY LIFE AND I'VE NEVER WON ANYTHING
WHAT STUFF?
WINALOT
RF

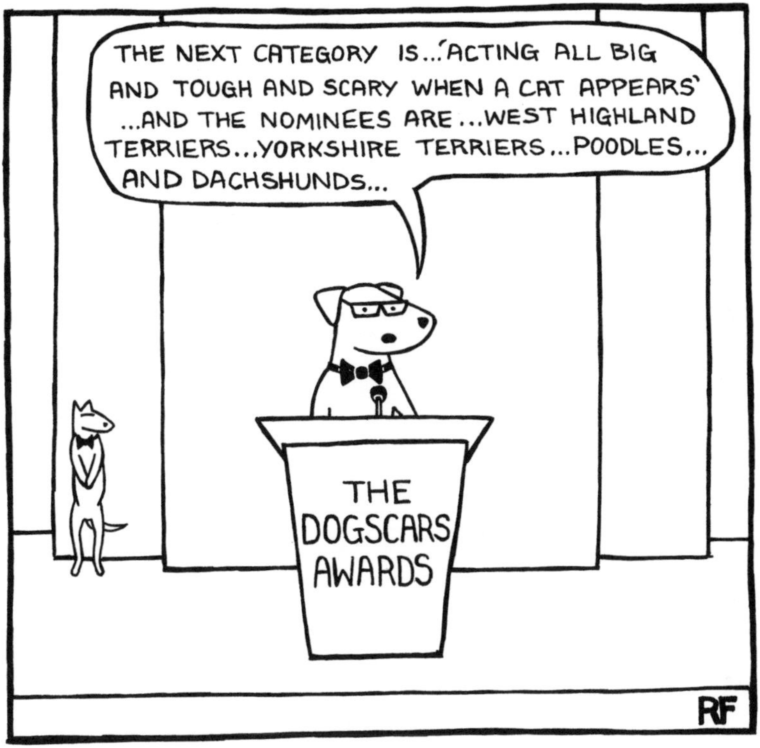
THE NEXT CATEGORY IS...'ACTING ALL BIG AND TOUGH AND SCARY WHEN A CAT APPEARS' ...AND THE NOMINEES ARE...WEST HIGHLAND TERRIERS...YORKSHIRE TERRIERS...POODLES... AND DACHSHUNDS...
THE DOGSCARS AWARDS
RF

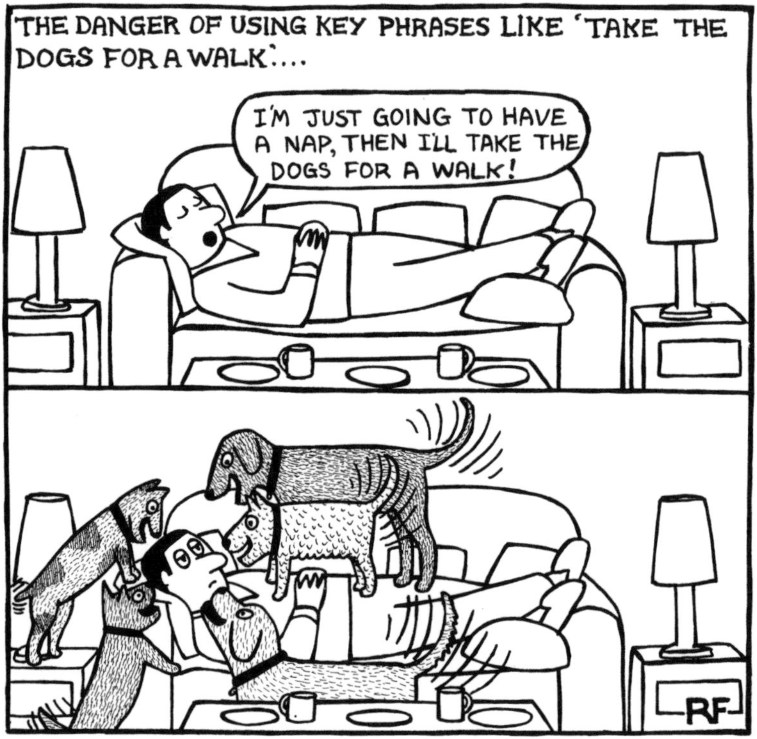
THE DANGER OF USING KEY PHRASES LIKE 'TAKE THE DOGS FOR A WALK'....
I'M JUST GOING TO HAVE A NAP, THEN I'LL TAKE THE DOGS FOR A WALK!
RF

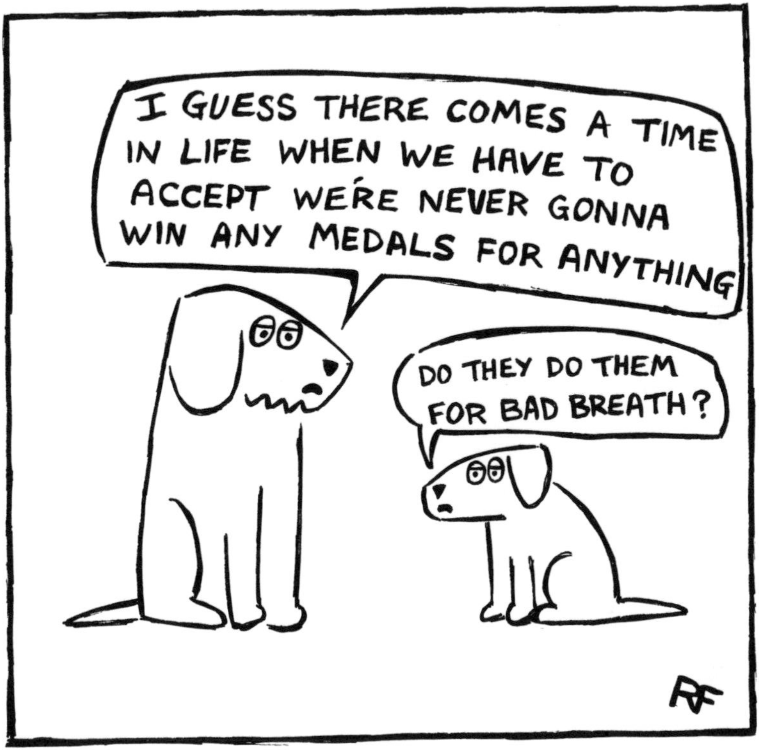
I GUESS THERE COMES A TIME IN LIFE WHEN WE HAVE TO ACCEPT WE'RE NEVER GONNA WIN ANY MEDALS FOR ANYTHING
DO THEY DO THEM FOR BAD BREATH?
RF

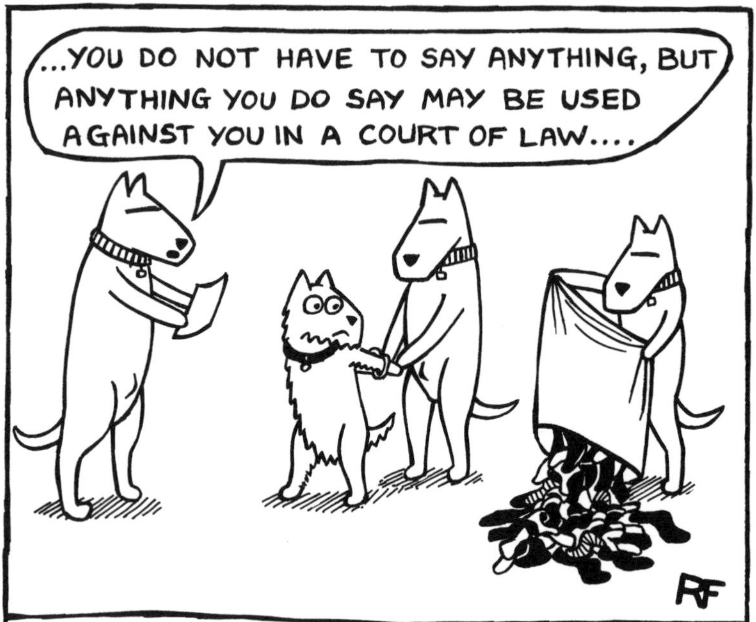
...YOU DO NOT HAVE TO SAY ANYTHING, BUT ANYTHING YOU DO SAY MAY BE USED AGAINST YOU IN A COURT OF LAW....
RF

SIDNEY'S YEARS OF SOCK STEALING FINALLY CAUGHT UP WITH HIM

DOGGY HOROSCOPES

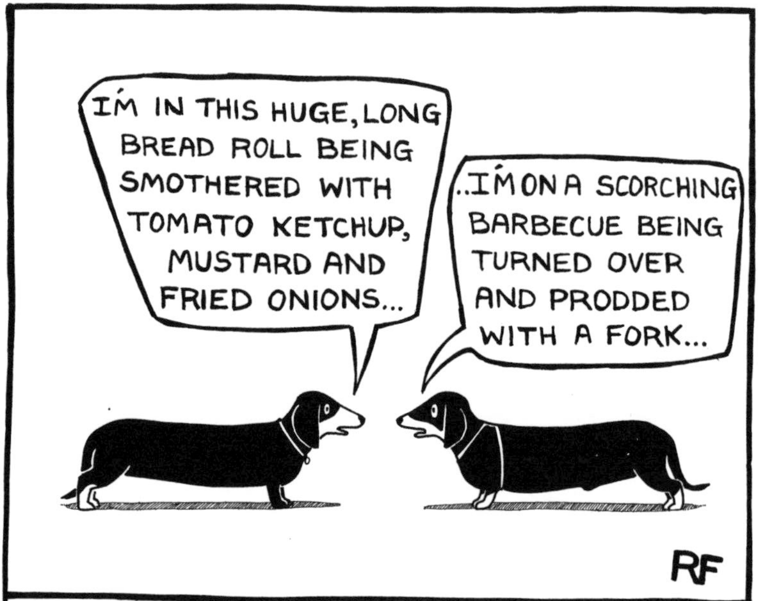
I'M IN THIS HUGE, LONG BREAD ROLL BEING SMOTHERED WITH TOMATO KETCHUP, MUSTARD AND FRIED ONIONS...
..I'M ON A SCORCHING BARBECUE BEING TURNED OVER AND PRODDED WITH A FORK...
RF

SAUSAGE DOG NIGHTMARES

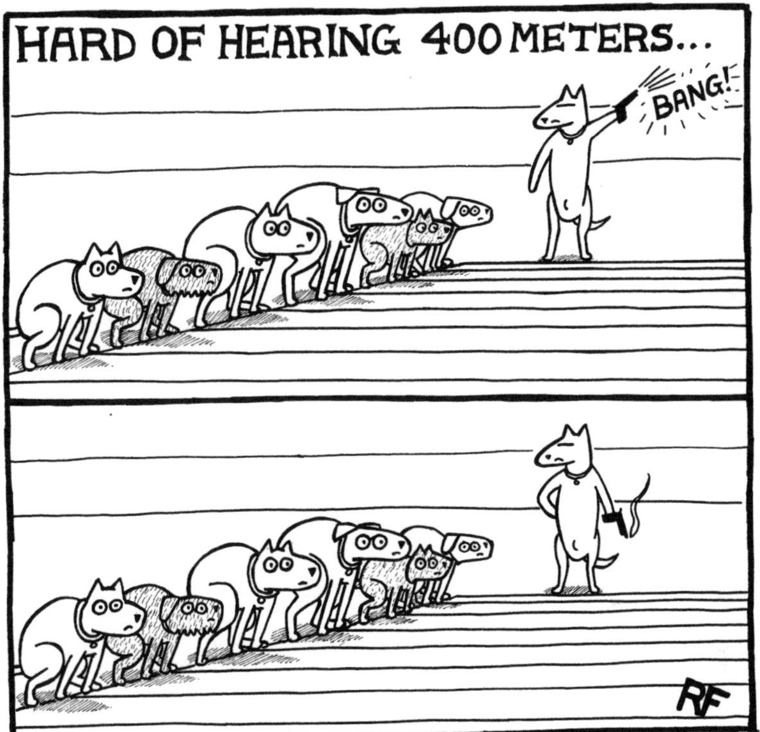
HARD OF HEARING 400 METERS...
BANG!
RF

93

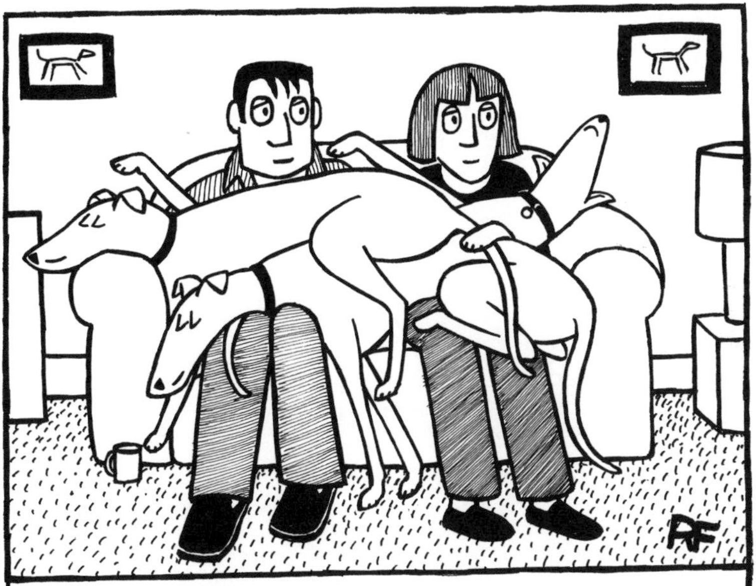
RF

BOB AND SUE LIKED NOTHING MORE THAN
A QUIET EVENING IN FRONT OF
THE TV WITH THE DOGS

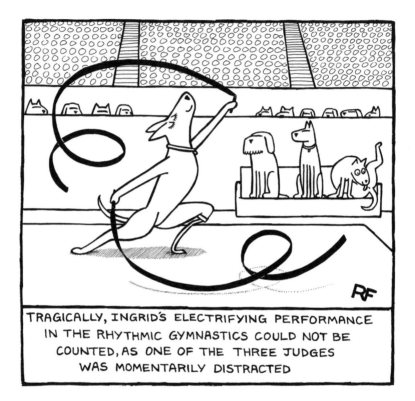

TRAGICALLY, INGRID'S ELECTRIFYING PERFORMANCE
IN THE RHYTHMIC GYMNASTICS COULD NOT BE
COUNTED, AS ONE OF THE THREE JUDGES
WAS MOMENTARILY DISTRACTED

PIDDLE!
PUDDLE!
WRIGGLE!
CUDDLE!
RF

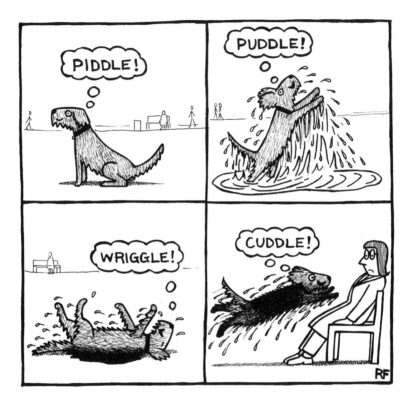

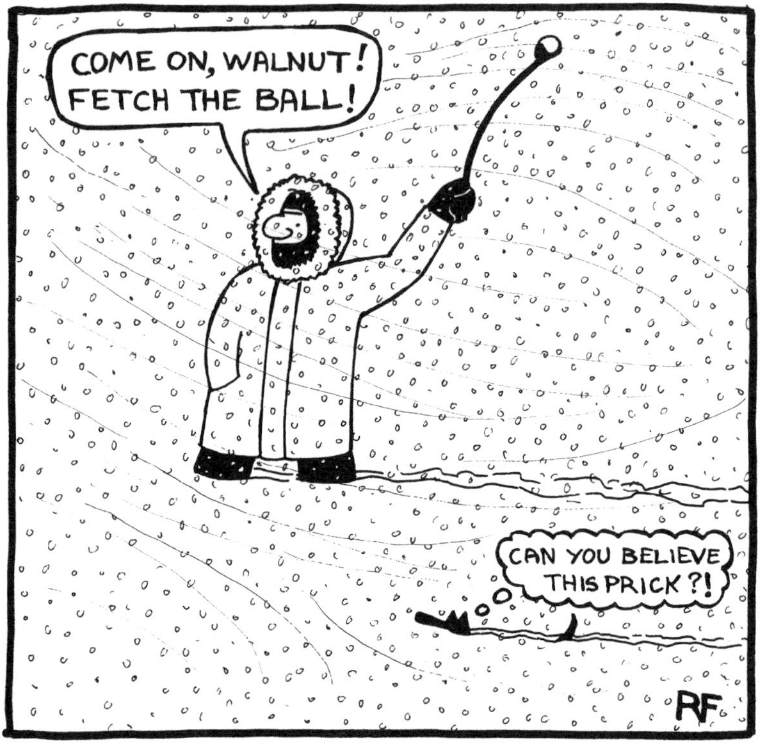
COME ON, WALNUT! FETCH THE BALL!
CAN YOU BELIEVE THIS PRICK?!
RF

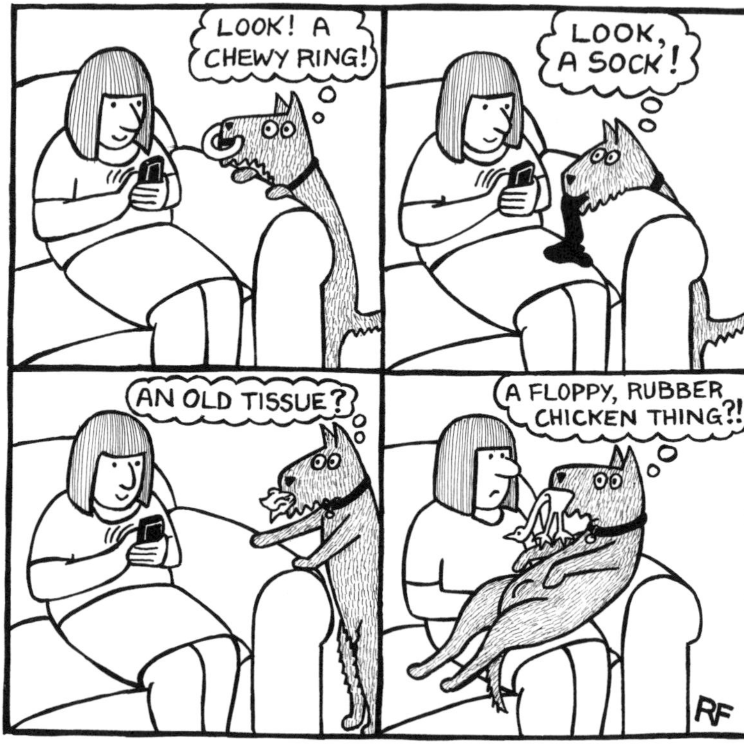
LOOK! A CHEWY RING!
LOOK, A SOCK!
AN OLD TISSUE?
A FLOPPY, RUBBER CHICKEN THING?!
RF

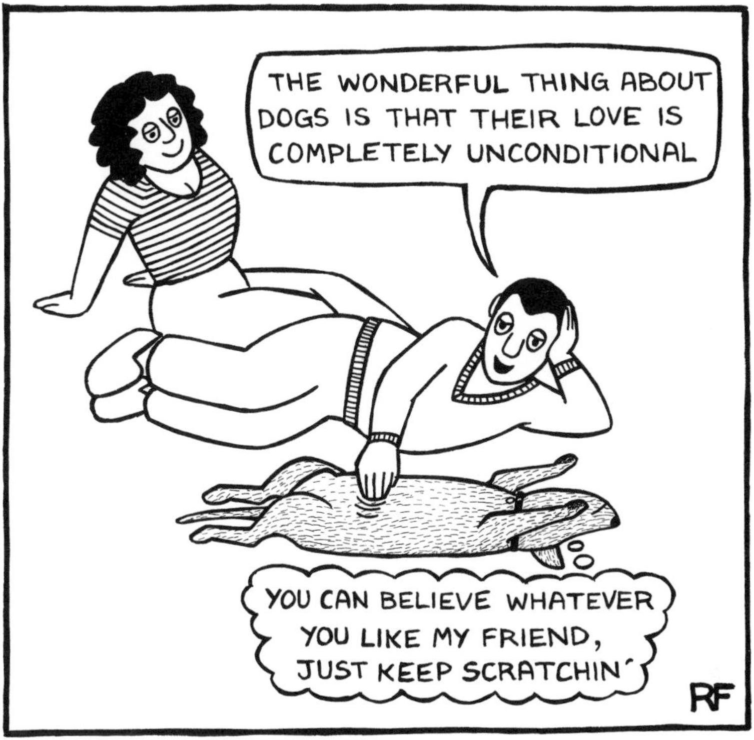
THE WONDERFUL THING ABOUT DOGS IS THAT THEIR LOVE IS COMPLETELY UNCONDITIONAL
YOU CAN BELIEVE WHATEVER YOU LIKE MY FRIEND, JUST KEEP SCRATCHIN'
RF

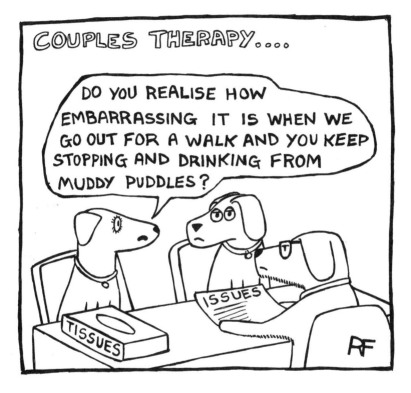

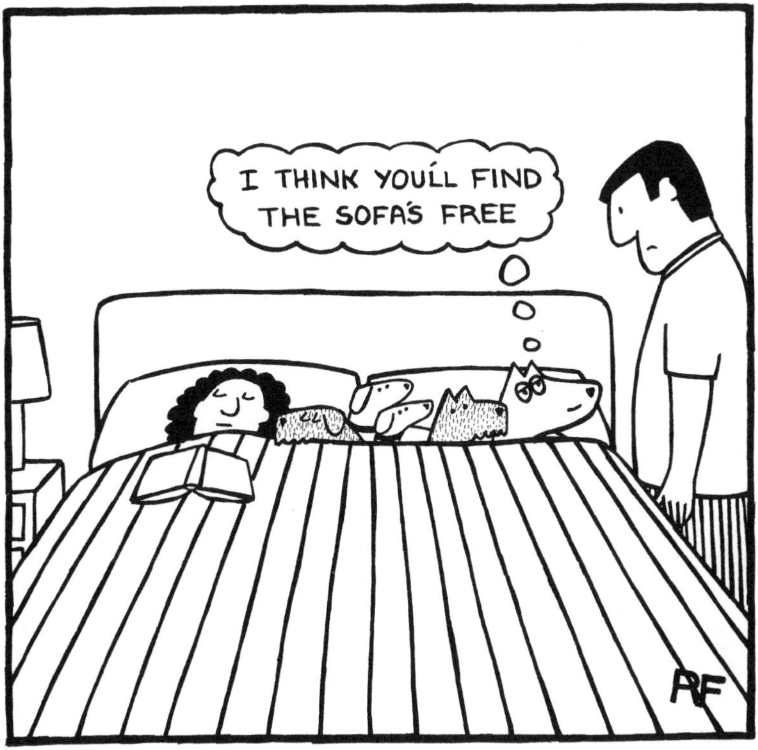
I THINK YOU'LL FIND THE SOFA'S FREE
RF

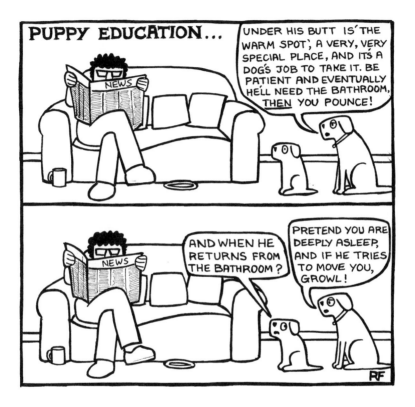

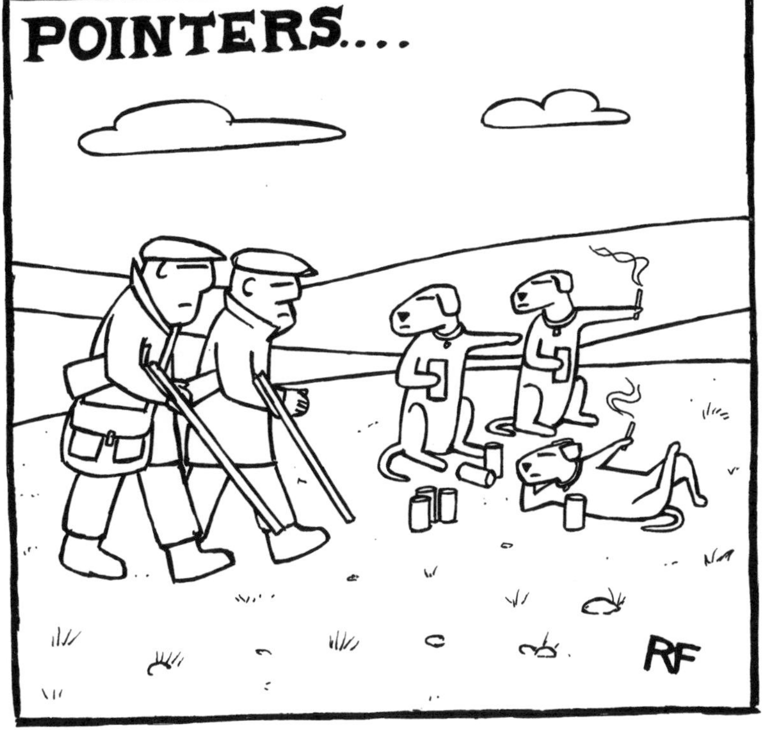
POINTERS....
RF

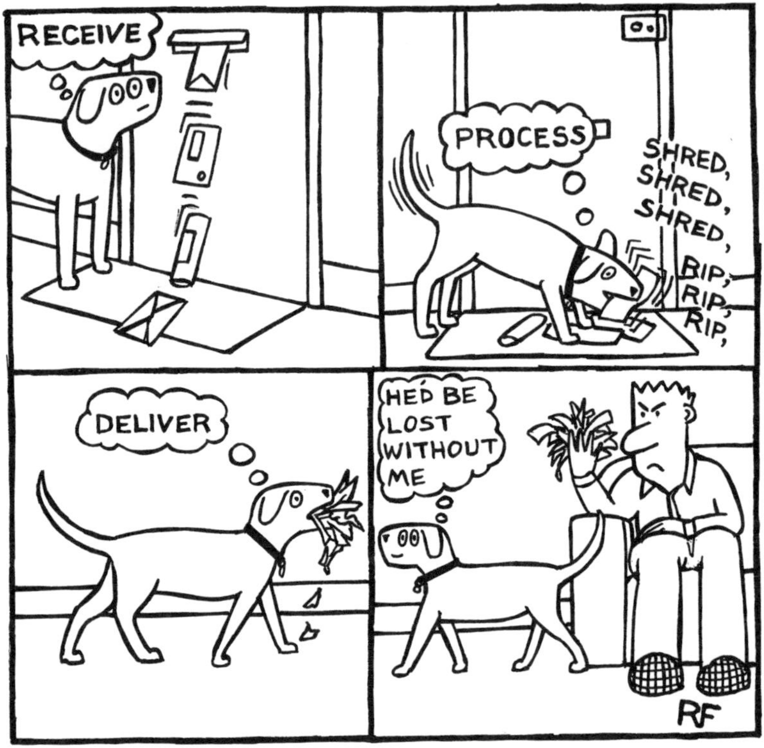
RECEIVE
PROCESS
SHRED, SHRED, SHRED,
RIP, RIP, RIP,
DELIVER
HE'D BE LOST WITHOUT ME
RF

VIVIEN CALLS THE DOG RESCUE
TEAM FOR THE SEVENTEENTH TIME

147

149

TILLY THE TERRIER SHARES HER STORY
AT BARKERS AND YAPPERS ANONYMOUS

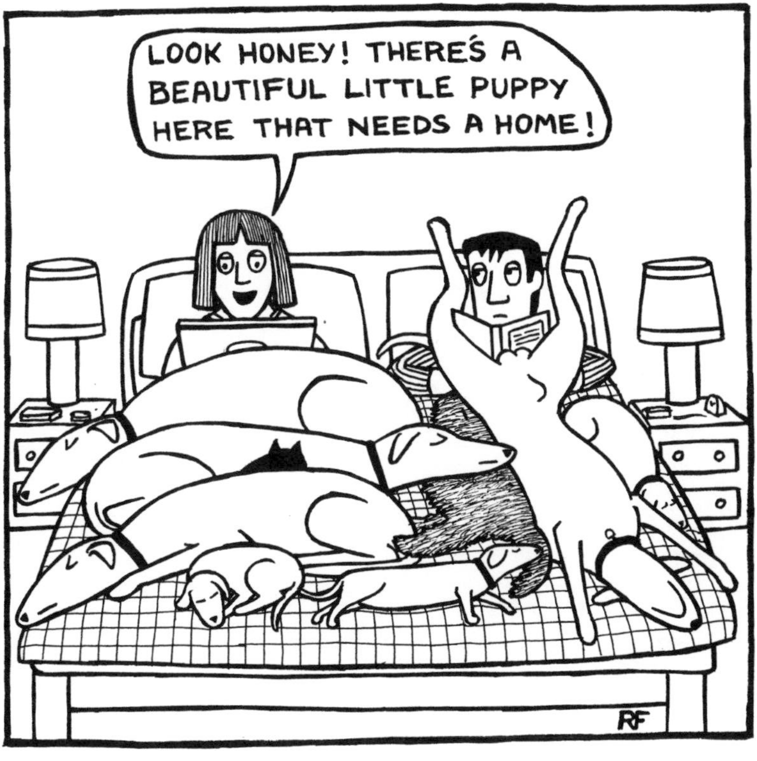
LOOK HONEY! THERE'S A BEAUTIFUL LITTLE PUPPY HERE THAT NEEDS A HOME!
RF

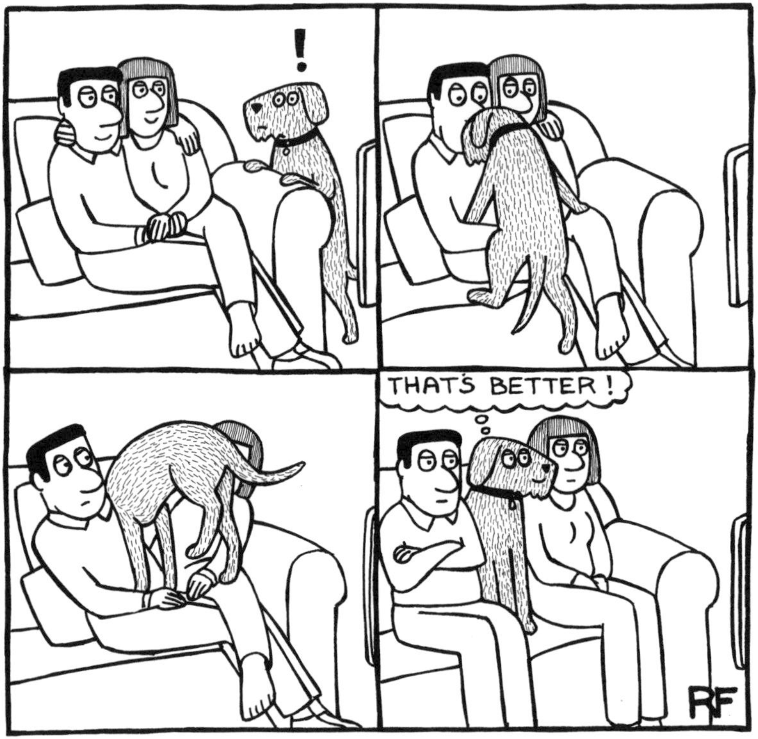
!
THAT'S BETTER!
RF

156

About the author

Rupert Fawcett became a professional cartoonist almost by accident when in 1989, whilst doodling, he drew a bald man in braces and carpet slippers and called him Fred. The Fred cartoons went on to be syndicated in the *Mail on Sunday* and published in several books. To date more than 9 million Fred greetings cards have been sold in the UK, Australia and New Zealand. Off The Leash is his latest creation.

www.rupertfawcettcartoons.com
www.facebook.com/OffTheLeashDailyDogCartoons